CW00820290

About the Author

Patricia Pizzey-Leeks is a respected clairvoyant medium and healer, beginning in 1973. She has travelled around East Anglia demonstrating her gifts, bringing comfort to people and proof of life after death of their loved ones. She served as President of Horley Spiritualist Association from 1990-2002. She helps others to develop their precious gifts of clairvoyance (clear sight) and healing. She very much still enjoys gardening – she used to enjoy driving but is no longer able to due to the macular degeneration of her eyes.

Dedicated to the memory of Miss R. E. Wardle – my teacher, friend and founder of the Horley Spiritualist Association. Also Chi – Running Bear –Joy –Young Silver – St Theresa of the Roses – all are angels of light.

Patricia Pizzey-Leeks

FETE OF MY SOUL

AUSTIN MACAULEY PUBLISHERS™

LONDON • CAMBRIDGE • NEW YORK • SHARJAH

ISBN 9781786935557 (Paperback)
ISBN 9781786935554 (E-Book)
www.austinmacauley.com

First Published (2018)
Austin Macauley Publishers Ltd.
25 Canada Square
Canary Wharf
London
E14 5LQ

Acknowledgements

Many thanks to Mrs. C. A. Windsor for permission to print the photo of Horley Spiritualist Church. Thank you to the dedicated team of workers at Austin Macauley Publishers Ltd. And to Peter R Worrow for transporting me to and from services.

In February 1985, our world fell apart when our daughter Louise, aged 19 years, was killed whilst walking over a crossing in London.

One moment, we had a loving, caring daughter, and in the next moment, we had lost her.

I felt immediately that, in fact, Louise had indeed moved to the next stage in life but, of course, could not understand this feeling.

We knew that we needed help to cope and decided to go to the local spiritualist church in St Ives, Cambs. There we met Pat, who was the visiting medium. The whole atmosphere was welcoming, and the service and clairvoyance were so uplifting.

After the service, my husband went to thank Pat, whereupon she described Louise, her age, her hair and her dress, and Pat said, "I know that she was more than a friend because I feel that I want to hug you." Pat also saw a fireman's helmet on my husband's head–yes, he was a fireman.

That was the start of our friendship. Pat must have helped many hundreds of people over many years. She was totally dedicated and so caring.

We moved away late 1988, so now 27 years later, we still keep in contact with Pat. She is a very special lady who has helped us to cope with life. We are blessed because Louise is still very much part of our lives.

Thank you, Pat.

Dinah and Albert

I first met Pat in 1990 after the loss of my father. I visited Horley Spiritualist Church where she was the president.

I was warmly welcomed by this lady, and as the weeks and months went by, Pat must have seen something in me, as she invited me to start sitting in her circle.

I had seen and felt spirit ever since I was a child but thought that everyone had this ability. I had never shared this with Pat, however, it was as if she already knew that. This lady took me under her wing, she taught me how to meditate, how to sit in my own truth, and how to trust spirit and the things that I was seeing and feeling in my young years (which, at times, was very confusing for me).

She gave me the foundations and the confidence to have personal responsibility with the things I was hearing and feeling as I started to open up to my awareness of the spirit world. She taught me to always be humble and work from the heart, with only the intention of using my gift to help others. Today, I am a well-known clairvoyant, medium and author, working up and down the country and abroad for over 25 years. But Pat really has been the wind beneath my wings; the teachings and foundations which this lady shared with me are priceless, making me the person I am today.

She silently sits in the background, never asking or needing recognition, but always giving herself to help anyone and everyone if they need it. She is and always will be, in my eyes, my earthly teacher. I owe this lady a great deal, and it is because of her teachings and guidance that I work in the way that I do today.

I can honestly say that in the last 27 years since I first met this lovely lady, and with the changes and challenges that come with life, she has never been judgemental and always been honest, truthful and supporting in all I do.

Thank you, Pat.

Stephanie Carr

Pat invited me to her home circle over 10 years ago, where she became my spiritual teacher and a dear, close friend.

We have shared much laughter and also many tears over the years together.

Pat has helped me in my development as a medium and has also given me a much better understanding of the beautiful spirit world that awaits us all.

There will always be a connection through the true power of love between us both.

Much love and light to a remarkable soul.

Richard Farthing

Pat's Life Story

Patricia Florence's earthly life began approximately at 6:30 am on the 18th December 1933 at the home of my parents, Edith Amy and Patrick John. This was Kentish Town, London N.W.5.

I was the first born of my parents. The cause of me writing this story came in the year 2002, when one January night as I lay in my bed, sobbing, for of late, I had not been able to control the tears. I cried out, "My God, my God! Why can I not stop these tears?"

And this lovely, calming voice said, "Child, the tide comes in, time and time again, until the beach is cleared of all the past rubbish and so it is with you. The tears will come until all the past hurts have been washed away."

I lay still, calm and truly amazed, yet I know when I think back that I should not have been amazed, for this voice—so calm and serene—had spoken to me before, which I will recall when I get to that part of my story, my life, as experienced by myself.

Maybe, by writing I may see what I need to learn and overcome all the tears.

As already stated, I was born in December 1933 in Kentish Town, London, NW5. We had a garden and I recall all my family relating how, at the age of 3 years, I loved packets of flower seeds—which Mum would buy me—that I planted. Somehow, I managed to get them growing in the correct order of height and apparently, created a beautiful garden. Pansies fascinated me; they have such dear little faces. To me, it's a miracle how such tiny little seeds grow into such beautiful flowers. To me, there really must be a far greater power of love; that which has not only created all of life, but continues to create and love us, never ever condemning us, for natural laws exist, such as: "*As you sow, so shall you reap*". In that way, I can see that we are our very own judges—for better or worse...

I loved music and my uncle Sid, my dad's brother, brought me a toy 'baby-grand piano', I can still see it in my mind's eye. I discovered that I could listen to a tune and simply play it without any music. I was about 4 years old when Mum said, "I must go shopping. If you are a good girl and look after your two brothers, Ted and Terry, I will bring you something nice on my way back."

I was very good. I kept them occupied well and truly; I gave them buckets and spades, and the ashes from the fireplace, plus water. Then, they made lovely castles on the squared lino. I cannot recall if Mum was cross or not, but I imagine that she was very upset; what a mess it must have caused. I was only interested in the wonderful gift that she brought me home. I was able to cuddle and love this wonderful ball of fur—my very first puppy dog—which I named Bobbie. He was an absolute bundle of joy, coloured black, brown, white, cream and gold. I loved him so much; a type of Collie cross, very fat and podgy. When Mum slept, so did Bobbie in my bed.

As he grew, he would protect my brothers and me. That is, if we attempted to cross the road whilst traffic still coming, he would haul us back to safety, by grabbing our coats in his teeth. I recall that my youngest brother Terry had a habit of running around with no pants or trousers on. He was still only a baby, needless to say that Bobbie was still only a puppy and anything wobbling around was a good target to test his teeth on. My brother wore pants from then on. Of course, Mum explained to him that Bobbie was really only playing and did not mean to hurt him.

Obviously, it did not turn brother Terry off of dogs, for in later life, he owned several of the most beautiful Alsatians I have ever seen. They were so very well trained.

We three children, i.e. Ted, Terry and me, really had a very happy child life. Mum taught us many things and always encouraged us to sing and play many different games. Dad worked in a green grocery shop. In his spare time, he built us a swing in the garden and also made us a tent.

My school was very close to our home. When Ted and Terry were old enough, they joined me there. At weekends, many relatives used to come and see us; grandparents, uncles and aunts, and quite often, we would all go to Regents Park where there were swings, roundabouts and slides to play on, plus sand pits, paddling pools and lakes where we could feed the ducks. And, of course, grass where we played cricket and ball games.

The London Zoo was also attached to Regents Park, so very often we could see some of the animals from there. We would always be treated to ice-cream by our family members.

After a day out to Regents Park, we would walk home and have a lovely family tea, then Uncle Sid would play the piano, and we would all have a lovely sing song; such very happy times. Other times, we would go by train to the seaside—south end was closest to us. Very pleasant times were spent there, with pony rides, paddling in the water, plus many different penny slot machines. I suppose, really, we were quite spoilt by grandparents and uncles and aunts, as we were the first grandchildren, nephews and nieces.

I had a great love for horses; whilst in south end, one could have rides on some, which I begged Mum to allow me to do. She said, "It will only walk round in a circle."

"No," I said, "he will let me gallop along the beach." But alas, Mum, as usual, was right. Round and round, he went in a circle...

December 23 1939, we had an early Christmas present in the form of a baby sister named Margaret June. Mum would nurse her on her lap, with Ted, Terry and me standing around her and singing the song: "Somewhere over the Rainbow". That song still stirs me to this day, and has quite a deep meaning to it. In fact, many years later, I used it as a theme when conducting a funeral service, in relation to a lady who had passed at a tender age of 39 years, whereby there were three young children to consider. Years still further on, this memory was brought back to me by a medium who I had never met. He described her in detail, how it was that she passed to a greater world and how the funeral service was conducted.

The 'Second World War' started on the 3rd September, 1939. So, suddenly, our world was turned upside down. We had to have black curtains fitted to all windows; this caused the Air Raid Warden to always be knocking at our door because children were always looking out of the windows, causing the light to show outside. Dad joined the Royal Air Force, and before we knew it, we children were on a railway station, together with our gas masks in little cardboard boxes and small suit cases. I can only remember the platform streaming with children and parents; the train seemed so big and long. We were waving and crying as we waved goodbye to our mums.

We arrived at a railway station in Wales, where we were lined up and escorted to a large building where we were allowed to take whatever food we wanted, plus milk or tea. After that, a lot of ladies and gentlemen came into the room, our names were called out; whereby, a lady came and took my hand and said: "Follow me, dear."

I tried to say to her, "But where are my brothers and baby sister?" but she did not seem to understand and just urged me on.

Where it was that I became separated from my brothers and baby sister, I do not know, but there, I was on my own. I was evacuated to somewhere in Wales. It was fairly close to Mount Snowden. I was billeted with a lovely lady and gentleman, who owned a newspaper shop with sweets etc. I, for the first time, had a bedroom to myself. I cried, for I missed my brothers as we all slept in the same room at home, and if they had bad dreams or cried, I was able to comfort them. Who would do that for them now? I was so worried about them.

I wondered if I would ever be able to see my mum, dad, grandma, granddad and my dear dog Bobbie again. Also, it was very frightening. The lady I was with, tucked me up in a single bed and suggested that she put my little bottle of nail varnish, which Grandma had given me, into the bathroom. If the fairies—who came at night—thought that I shouldn't wear it until I was older, they would carry it away, but if it was okay to wear it, it would be there in the morning. Yes, you have guessed it. It was gone in the morning. I missed my Bobbie, my mum, dad, grandma, granddad, my brothers and my baby sister, even though the lady and gentleman were so kind and loving.

Fortunately, they had a little Terrier dog that they let me dress up in my black doll's clothes; he was so docile like my Bobbie. I had my 6th birthday in Wales. There's a picture of me, standing at the bottom of Mount Snowden. Out of the blue, I was packed off once again with gas mask and a little case and no nail varnish or dogs this time.

Apparently, the powers of the day endeavoured to keep families together, so I was transported to the corner house, Stourton, Shipston on Stour, Warwickshire, where I was reunited with my brothers Ted and Terry and baby sister Peggie (Margaret). The lady and gentleman who said goodbye to me were sad, as they had no children of their own. We had all got on so well. Sadly, I cannot recall their names or the address.

Two ladies lived in the thatched cottage at Stourton, who we were to call Mammy Clarke and Aunty Mary. They had a Jersey Cow, also named Mary, who had large brown eyes. They had something like a small holding, with hens, cockerel, ducks, geese, plus orchard and large barn, plus a front and rear garden. The toilet was at the top of the garden, where we had squares of newspaper for toilet paper.

Mammy Clarke was very strict, but she loved my baby sister who, like my youngest brother, had lots of blonde curls. Actually, she wanted to adopt her, but Mum would not allow that. However, many years later, Mum told me that Mammy Clarke did adopt another little girl. So, I guess some good came out of the war years.

Life there was quite a mixture. I loved the country side, but being the eldest, I was to look after my brothers and sister and another lad called Malcolm. Whatever any of them did wrong, I was in trouble for that and was sent to bed with no tea or supper, not even a drink. Across the road from the thatched cottage that had a stone wall around it, on a patch of grass was a wooden seat where we would hold our little concerts and sing our hearts out.

We did what was known as War Effort, which was picking baskets of blackberries, rosehips—made into rosehip syrup as Vitamin C for babies—peas, potatoes and mushrooms. A gentleman with a lorry would call every so often to take all we had gathered and take it onto London, and we would be given a certificate stating how much we earned.

We had our own little den in a field and a broken tree that looked like a horse, which we would ride. I can remember Mum coming to see us on one occasion when I begged her to come and see our den and horse. Bless her; she was petrified of cows and didn't want to cross a field where they were to get to our den. I assured her that she was safe and they would not come near her. Poor Mum, as soon as she stepped in the field, lo and behold, the cows headed for her. Nope, no way would she see our den.

A little river also ran through that field, where we gathered water cress to use in sandwiches. I remember that on one occasion, the boys and I reached into a rabbit hole and took the babies back to the cottage. Dearie me, was I in trouble; back to bed, no food or drink and return the dear, little rabbits the next day. I've often thought that how cruel it was of us to take those babies from their mum. I hope that she didn't abandon them.

Another time, we were walking through meadow grass and a mouse ran up my trouser leg. My brothers and friends thought that highly funny. I was petrified but got the giggles, as it tickled.

On another occasion, one of my brothers lost his Wellington boot; it slipped off into the river. We tried everything to get it but to no avail. We were always told to stay away from the river, so we dared not tell that is where we lost it, and we said, "It got stuck in a rabbit hole and we could not pull it out." My goodness, the mind boggles now as to what possibly could have happened.

At one stage during the war, lots of tanks, army lorries and motor cycles trundled through the village; they were on their way to eventually go abroad. The soldiers gave us letters to post for them. The village people took one at a time, down to post office, I do not know why. My brothers and I collected lots of them and then took them to post office. We were rich for a while from the coins given to us by the soldiers.

We would hear Mr Winston Churchill speaking on the radio, also Princess Elizabeth. The radio was powered by accumulator battery. As we did not have electricity, the battery had to be topped up every now and again. I would pray every night for the safe return of my dad from South Africa and then India; he was an aircraft mechanic in the Royal Air Force. And also for Uncle Sid, who is my father's brother and was in the Middle East, and Uncle Jimmy, who is my mum's brother and was a kind and very caring soul. Later, he was killed near London Bridge; he had kindly changed duties for a friend. Poor Uncle Jim had only been married for a week to Aunt Anne.

My wonderful uncle Sid—known affectionately as Uncle Tiny—was a Grenadier Guardsman but was captured in Germany and imprisoned in Stalag 13 prison. He, too, was my mum's brother. Uncle Ted was in Royal Navy. He was Aunt Rose's husband, who was Mum's sister. Mum and her two sisters Rose and Queenie were all in the A.T.S. Mum—bless her—was drummed out of that for silent insubordination, that is showing her thoughts by her large brown eyes. She then joined the auxiliary fire service. Of course, I also prayed for both sets of grandparents and great aunts and uncles, all left in London, and my beloved dog Bobbie. My mother's mother remarried a gentleman called Ted and lived in a cottage in Middle Road, Lytchett Matravers, near Poole, Dorset, and became known as Nanny and granddad.

I missed my dog Bobbie so much that one night, when praying for his safety, I actually saw him by my bed. Instinctively, I felt that he had died, though I prefer the word passed, so I wrote to Mum, asking if he was okay. She assured me that he was, but eventually when I went home, she had to tell me the truth: Poor Bobbie had passed to a happier world.

One night, when the siren went off, Mum and Bobbie set off for the underground (where people slept whilst air-raids were on). As they left the house, Mum said, "Oh, Bobbie, I've forgotten my handbag." So—bless him—he went back to get it. As he did so, the lintel of the door fell on him and caused his passing to the greater world. I continued to see him many times and had to believe that perhaps he was dreaming that he was with me. The truth was that it was my first psychic experience.

Again, in later years, I was given messages regarding my "Bobbie"; the mediums, explaining his size and colouring, plus his name. Wonderful to know that even our animals continue to live on in a greater world. I remember only seeing my dad twice during the war. On one occasion, he stood by the stone wall that surrounded the thatched cottage in Warwickshire, and I can still hear my brother, Terry, saying "Are you my daddy?" in a very deep broad voice.

Another time, when we came out of school, there he was, waiting for us. On both occasions, he was wearing his Royal Air Force uniform, quite a sight really, for all to see. As we lived in the countryside and I don't think many people had relations in the services, they would have been exempt due to agriculture needs. Even Mum only came a couple of times. On one occasion, it took her all night to find us as due to the war, there was a complete blackout at night and no direction signs were available. This was so that the enemy would not know where they were.

At school, we were taught by the headmaster's wife and wives of other teachers, for they were all male in those days, and male teachers had to go to war. Only conscientious objectors were exempt, one such was my uncle George, who was put in prison for having those kinds of thoughts; I admired him for doing what his conscience told him. Actually, the headmaster had a beautiful old car but new in those days. It was locked in an old barn. We children had a lovely time in that and were never once caught. The horn was on the outside of the car, something like Mary Poppins' car. It's a wonder that we were not heard by someone. I do hope that we didn't do any harm to it, but we did enjoy our times in it.

I hated school, I think mostly because I was wrapped over the knuckles with a ruler, for using my left hand. I couldn't help it; I was left handed, but really, it did not do me any harm, for now, I can use both hands. We would go apple scrumping, eat hawthorne berries and leaves from the hedgerows; we called the latter bread and cheese.

On one occasion, we watched a cow give birth to a calf and were enjoying stroking the calf when an Italian prisoner of war, who worked on the farms, saw us and gave us a good telling off. He said that it was possible that the mother cow could kill us. She didn't of course, and probably knew that we were only children. However, we never did it again.

Leaflets were dropped by German Aircrafts, stating that when Germany would win the war, all dark-haired people and children would be killed.

My brother Ted and I were scared stiff that Hitler might win the war, as the propaganda was that he would kill all those who had dark hair; Ted's was dark brown and mine, black. The Germans would drop leaflets from their aircrafts, stating those ideas that was a real fear for us.

The villagers, especially children (although, I suspect in hind sight that they got it from their parents), did not like us Londoners. I was tall and very thin, especially my legs, so I was called match-stick legs. They might have been so, but those legs showed our country friends what they could do when it came to Sports Day, for I won every race that I went into. Only the greatest power of love saw that, as we had no one to come and see us on our big days.

My brother Ted and I used to go to the house next to the school, which was headmaster's house, to do their gardening and I loved that. Actually, one Christmas, Ted was Joseph, and I, our Lady Mary in the Nativity play held at the school. I was so very proud to play that part. It was very special for me. Again, there was no one there, who knew us, to watch us (I was christened as a Roman Catholic). Sweets were on ration during the war so we silly children bought ex-lax for chocolate; it didn't do us any harm. My sister Peggy—still a baby—was somewhat a pain in the butt; always demanding things.

Once, she saw Ted and me smoking rolled-up paper and once again reported to Mammy Clarke. Off I went, only me, to bed; no tea or supper, not even a drink. In later years, I found myself punishing myself by not eating when my husband or anyone else was cross with me (Strange, what the mind does to one).

The next day, I had to take sister Peggie with us out to play, in her big, bassinet pram. I am very ashamed now to say that I, very deliberately, let her pram go down a hill on its own. Fortunately, there was a set of bars that protected folks from falling into a small ditch/stream. Poor Peggy was screaming but did behave for a little while after that.

As Peggie grew, I had the task of washing and dressing her. She was a real monkey who used to scream and say that I was hurting her. When it came to combing her lovely, curly hair, it was sheer murder. On Sundays, we were made to go to Church of England; Sunday School first, then morning service at 11 am and evening song at 6:30 pm. Brothers Ted and Terry were in the choir. I was naughty. I made them giggle by crooking my finger, harmless fun really. But I always got a conscience afterwards, as we were taught that God was watching everything we did (Now, of course, I see God in a totally different light. He/She is in all things that I see, do, hear, sense, smell; all of the creations and within my own being; and is a perfect love, who condemns not and gives us free will to do exactly as we choose, as a natural law exists that states, '*As you sow, so shall you reap*'. Hence, we punish ourselves). I was taught to ring the Bells at church

24

and loved doing that, one set of peels to call people to the church and one to state that service was over.

Every morning, we were given by Mammy Clarke a cube of sugar, soaked in TCP, to eat; it was supposed to prevent colds. Whether it did or not, I cannot say, as we rarely ate it. We put it behind the black horse-hair-filled settee, called Chaise Lounges, which stood on a stone floor. Actually, to this very day, I still smell TCP, if and when a cold is about to take place. They must never have swept behind there, for we were never caught.

When the war ended during 1945 (six long years we were parted from our family), we held a concert on our seat in the triangle opposite the cottage. We sang 'God Save the King (then King George 6th) you are my Sunshine' and many other war-time songs, like 'Roll out the Barrel', 'Run Rabbit run run run, we are the Ovalteenies' etc.

We were so excited that at last it was all over and we would be able to go home and be with Mum and Dad. But no, that was not to be, as our London home had been bombed. That's when my dog, Bobbie, was killed. After the war, we discovered that grandma had sent us many parcels, containing sweets etc., but we had never received them.

I cannot remember how it came about, but at one stage during the war, we went by train to London. The guard took charge of us. I went to the toilet during this journey, only to find the door had locked itself and I could not get out. I was terrified and was sure that I would never see my brothers again, but eventually, I was missed and the guard came and let me out. I still leave all toilet doors open, in case I get locked in.

Once in London, we stayed for a while with Mum at Leighton Rd Kentish Town N.W.5. On our first night there, a doodle bug came over and Mum made us all hide under the table. I heard her praying, "Dear Lord, I'm so sorry that I brought them home. Please, please, protect them."

Suddenly, we heard the engine of the doodle bug stall, and Mum said, "It's going to be okay, for it will glide for about a mile and then come down."

I believe it was the one that hit a bus that careered onto the top of some flats in Harrington St Mornington Crescent, near Euston Station. My Aunt Ginny and Uncle George lived down that road. Uncle George was in prison for being a conscientious objector to war.

Whilst we were still in London, I was ill. I believe I had the first bout of three lots of measles. I can still remember my dear granddad bringing me daffodils, which was wonderful and made me feel so grown up. I can still see them in my mind's eye, sitting on top of my cabinet bed; it was a bed that folded up into a cabinet and looked like a small wardrobe when folded. I received a receipt for all the war effort in collecting foods to be sent to London. It amounted to £9.50. Bless her, Mum had to keep it to buy a radio.

Apparently, Mum could only rent Leighton Rd, Kentish Town for a short time, so we were shipped off again, this time to Nanny. My mum's mother lived in an old thatched cottage in Middle Rd, Lytchett Matravers, near Poole, Dorset. Of course, it was all done to protect us children but we did feel somewhat abandoned. As already stated, our real home in London had been bombed. We soon settled into our new life.

Granddad was a character, he laid hedges for a living and used to make them look wonderful. Every evening, he went to the chequer's public house for a pint or two, or maybe more. In time, I used to baby sit the landlady's children. If I remember correctly, I believe her surname was Bourne. Granddad was a really good gardener and all our vegetables came from his garden. The soil was jet black, for each time that he emptied the 'Elson' bucket from outside the toilet, he would place it on compost heap, which then in time, he would dig it into the garden soil.

The front garden was very long, with a path leading down to bottom gate. Just outside the cottage was a well, from which I had to draw the water we used for cooking, washing ourselves, washing up, bathing in a tin bath in front of the fireplace, washing clothes—which I did, again, in a tin bath outside of kitchen door and put clothes through a wooden mangle, not much, needed ironing after going through the mangle.

To draw the water from the well, the knack was to throw the bucket, which was on a long rope, open end down first, and then haul it up by the rope. To the right of the garden path was Mickey, the dog, and his kennel. He appeared to be vicious, but this was only really with strangers. He ate same food as we did, plus a bowl of bread and raw tea. At bottom on the right were plum trees, Victoria and black plums.

Along both sides of garden path were blackcurrant bushes, 24 in all, a few yards from cottage door was a rose arch, covered in beautiful pink roses, and to the left of garden was a small flower bed. From there to the bottom of the garden, it was all vegetables: potatoes, different types of cabbage, runner beans, broad beans, onions and shallots, Brussel sprouts. Every year, granddad would change vegetables about, i.e. cabbages where potatoes were etc.

Another path led from front to back of left-hand side of the garden, and around back of the cottage, where outside toilet was, also compost heaps, Marrow and Cucumber beds.

And a couple of apple trees; one for cooking and one for eating. The latter were small but very sweet. To the right-hand side of the cottage, as we faced it, was a lean too, built on side of cottage, and the girls' bedroom was next to that. From inside of bedroom were narrow, winding stairs up to my brothers' bedroom.

The lean to became quite handy for boys and me, for it led out to the garden, and when such things as the Fair came to the village—which we were not allowed to go to—we would creep out, down the garden and off to enjoy the Fair. On one such occasion, we had just got inside the garden and had to hide by the plum trees as granddad came in, a bit worse for the drink. He stood right close to us and did a tiddle in the hedge, which was scary. We were choking ourselves from trying not to laugh. How we were never caught, I'll never know.

Next to the girls' bedroom was the lounge, kitchen and dining area; all in one small room. We had no electricity so we had to use oil lamps and candles. There was no sink, just a washing up bowl on a small table. There was a range fire with oven attached to it, which I used to love blacking and polishing to a high shine. That's where Nanny cooked all our lovely meals. She used to let us have a cup of cabbage water whilst it was cooking on the hob. With salt and pepper added to it, it was wonderful.

Nanny also baked apple tarts, rhubarb and custard and made delicious blackcurrant jam and plum jam. Next to the fireplace was a cupboard which reached from ceiling to the floor, Wee Wee, the cat, always had her kittens in there. All Nanny's cats had funny names, one such was Futters, I guess Nanny had quite a sense of humour.

On either side of the fireplace were fireside chairs, one for Nanny and one for Granddad. When he was out, I would sit in his chair and look at the lovely face of Nanny. She was thin but elegant, had long black hair that she could sit on when hanging down long, but every day, she plaited it in one long plait and wrapped it around into a bun with waves to the right hand side of her head. She had beautiful, blue eyes. I would sit and listen to her for hours.

I remember her telling me how when she gave birth to Uncle Tiny, her husband and young daughter of 14 years, both of whom had only died a few days before, came and stood at her side whilst she gave birth. To me, that was absolutely natural. It was not until later years that I realised how wonderful that was. She must have known that I had the same gift as her.

Next came the wooden table and dining chairs. The table had to be scrubbed every day. On the other side of table and chairs was a Welsh dresser and a door leading to Nanny and Granddad's bedroom with just one rug in front of the fire place, which was made of strips of material woven through a canvas. This had to be taken outside and shaken each day. There was no electricity, we used to have an oil lamp with a glass funnel, and I used to love hearing Nanny's ring, tinkling the glass as she cleaned the glass tower.

We had candles to show our way when we went to bed. Wee Wee, the cat, had many kittens; most were found homes, but sometimes I believe that Granddad had to put them to sleep; they were heart-breaking times. The cat was a wonderful mother; she would bring home live baby rabbits to teach her kittens how to catch them for food. Granddad also had two ferrets to help him catch rabbits for our dinner since there were no unnatural rabbit deaths in those days.

Next to our cottage was Tong's farm. We were allowed to help the farmer during the school holidays. We helped him with the harvest by stacking the sheaths of corn into a tent like shape, then gleaning heads of loose corn ears to feed the chickens with. We also enjoyed hay making and milking the cows. And across the road from cottage, on a fine day, we could see across the fields and into the distance "Corfe Castle"; I used to imagine that was where the war used to be.

Once settled, I loved living with Nanny. I would sit opposite her when Granddad was not there, looking at her beautiful, blue eyes. She was a very attractive lady. She was very thin and always wore a wrap over overall—unless she was going out, then she looked elegant, with coat and matching hat, handbag, shoes and gloves, together with a handkerchief soaked in Yardley's Lavender water. She cooked wonderful meals and things like rhubarb pie, apple pies and apple and blackcurrant pies. Bless her, she smoked just like I do, but she managed 60 Star cigarettes a day which cost pence in those days not pounds; cost eight pennies for ten cigarettes.

Every evening, I had to listen to the radio racing results and mark off against the newspaper, the first three in every race. Nan's newspaper was the Daily Herald and Granddad's, the Daily Mail. He was a conservative and Nan was a labour voter. Yes, you might guess it there was some lively conservation. The radio was run on an accumulator battery, which every now and again I had to take to a shop and have it topped up.

Every morning, Nan and Granddad would pick out the horses that they wanted to back, from their newspapers, then Granddad would take them to the chequer's public house and give them to what was known in those days as a 'runner' and then collect any winnings the next day. Granddad was quite lucky; he mostly backed favourites. In those days, it was illegal to bet and if a runner was caught, they could get a very large fine.

The postman always called in for a cup of tea and a chat. As did Aunt Rose—my mum's sister. She had lovely ginger curly hair, was small and petite, had a great sense of fun, and good humour. Her husband, Uncle Ted, was still away in the navy. They had a son, our cousin, again named Ted. He was quite spoilt but was okay when in a good mood. I used to fight with him, trying to stick up for my brother Ted—who was thin as opposed to cousin Ted.

Our nan also read the tea leaves, which is something I later learnt to do, but now I know that it is only a concentration point. We went to school; it was a lot better there and we had a real headmaster. We all liked him, he had two sons; one, I remember, was named Peter. He played in the school's football team. We also had an art teacher, who also doubled as a sports master; some of the girls would fall head over heels in love with him, others thought that he fancied himself. To me, he was a teacher; that was all.

Once, I remember, we had to do a futuristic drawing. I painted a large lounge/sitting room. It had a lovely white fireplace surround and a television on the wall in the corner. How or why I did that, I do not know, as in those days, televisions were not about. That was approx. 1945 and I was 12 years old. The room also had a large patio door, again not around then (But years later, in fact 1990, I lived in that room at Horley Manse, London Rd. Ipswich. Suffolk, when I became president and resident medium of Horley Spiritualist Assn; Church, 345 London Rd. Ipswich. IP2 OBG).

At the school that we attended in Lytchett Matravers, Dorset. We had a coke burner that was round and an approximately 3-feet-high fire container. In winters, the milk which was for everyone, was in a bottle 1/3rd of a pint each. In winter, the cream on top of milk would freeze and stand out about 1" above top of the bottle. When I was on milk duty, I loved that. Needless to say that not many children got the cream because I, the naughty girl, had finished it.

My desk was near to the coke burner so it was nice during winter. I was very skinny so I guess that the teachers thought that I needed to stay warm. We had dinners at school too; they also were very good. I think we all enjoyed living with Nanny, even though she was very strict. We would go with Farmer Tonga's workers when the corn was cut and help to stack the corn sheaths, and go gleaning for any loose ears of corn to feed chickens with. We also went hay making, plus stacking the hay.

I once threw a pitch fork into a hay stack, and it came back down and stuck in my leg; I still have the scar. Once when taking hay to put into cow's feeders, I came across a mouse nest and took a couple home to show my mum, who was visiting us at the time. What a commotion I caused! I told my mum to close her eyes as I had a surprise for her, "It won't hurt me, will it?" she said.

"No, Mum, of course not," said I. Well, dearie me, when she opened her eyes and went berserk. Poor Mum was petrified. I really thought that she would love the dear, little creatures. I was taught how to milk the cows and used to milk them quite often, that would not do for my mum, and eh, I don't know these townies.

We used to have fun while walking through the woods. In those days, we were allowed to pick the flowers. There were carpets of primroses, bluebells, and wild daffodils. Nanny always had flowers for Mother's Day and for her birthday, which was 16th April. There were also blue and white coloured violets in the woods. We were taught at school the names of many wild plants. Somewhere in the woods, my boyfriend Lesley and I carved our initials in the shape of a heart on an oak tree. There was also an old manor house which was supposed to be haunted. We children visited it one day, but it scared the living day light out of us, and we never went near it again.

Occasionally, when the weather was very dry, no one would be able to draw water from the well. Then, we had to collect it from the village pump, just up the road from our home. Mrs Legg's shop was also in that area. She would have large, square biscuit tins which contained oranges, apples, plums, other vegetables, and also loose biscuits and cheese that was not wrapped. She had to cut off the amount of cheese that a person wanted. The oranges had tissue paper wrapped around each one, with the emblem of the country they came from. We kept scrap books with these pasted in them.

I loved Nan so much. She wasn't at all happy living in Dorset, nor was she with my step-grandfather, so I saved my pocket money and bought her all the week's shopping for her birthday so that she could use her pension to catch a train to London. Dear me, what had I done. She cried so much—apparently, she was so surprised that someone would do that for her. Mind you looking at it now, what a silly girl I was; who would look after us if she went?

Returning to the time, I had to do the washing and put it through the mangle. If anything did have to be ironed, then flat irons would be placed in front of the fire to heat up and one spat on it to ensure it was hot enough to use. There was no ironing board in those days; just a folded blanket and sheet placed on the table.

On winter evenings, my nan, grandfather, brothers, Ted and Terry, sister Peggie and I used to play 'Snakes and Ladders', Domino's, Tiddly Winks, Drafts, Cards, etc. Poor Nan was a bad loser; she—bless her—hated losing. I used to have to make the boys' beds and the girls' beds, and clean both rooms. The mattresses were made of feathers and had to be shaken up well, otherwise they would become lumpy and difficult to sleep on. When I think back, I really had to work quite hard for a child but I guess it stood me in good stead for life.

Occasionally, I would have to go to Morden to stay and look after an aunt who was often ill due to gastric ulcer and I did not mind doing that. On one occasion, she had given birth to a baby son, and there was I, singing away and throwing down the stairs all the dirty sheets, right on top of the vicar, poor man. My aunt's husband was a farm labourer. He had to get up very early to go and milk the cows. He would bring a cup of tea into my bedroom for me and fondled me.

The first time, it was such a shock, and I was told not to tell anyone. I worried all day long about it. The next day, he did it again. This time, I decided that I would go back home to my nan, but if I told anyone about it, it could cause so much pain, not only to my aunt but it may cause a break up in the family, and of course, he would probably deny it. So, I walked, what to me seemed miles, to get back to Nan's.

On the way, I picked wild strawberries to eat. When I got there, my mum—bless her—was there too. They all kept asking what was wrong, but I just could not say; it would have caused a lot of pain. So, I just said that I did not want to go back. That evening, my uncle came to fetch me, and I just cried and said, "I would not go back. I want to stay with Nan and Mum." I suspect that my nan had guessed, for she did not force me to go back and I was so grateful.

I was never pressed again to go back there, thank God, and I always avoided him when he visited Nan's. Why men can be so disloyal to their wives, I'll never know, or why they think they can treat a child in that way, goodness knows. I often wonder now that how at such a young age did I know that it was wrong of him to do such things, however somehow, I did know. Thank God. It was a scary experience. Other than that episode, I loved being with my nan.

I was a real tomboy. I used to ride my bike around a dirt track, trying to race the boys, and it was all just good fun. But Granddad—bless him—could not understand how I got so many punctures. My brother Ted was a rascal. One day, we were playing at the back of the cottage when he said to me, "Go and ask Nan for some bread and jam."

"No," said I, "you do it yourself."

"Well," he said, "if you do not, I'll tell Nan that you have a boyfriend called Lesley." So, off I went three times in all. Well, if it was dry, wet, or snow, cottage door was always open. After the third time, Nan threw the loaf at me; it missed and went into a puddle. I just ran, but—bless her—she never seemed to hold a grudge. When I used to go and buy Nan a loaf, it was always so nice and fresh that I could never resist taking a pinch of it from the corner. All Nan ever said was: "Mrs Legg has some mighty big mice in her shop."

One year, we had a great deal of snow; I think it was about 1947. We could not go to school as we could not even get out of the cottage, as the snow piled right up and over the top of the door. It was so dark indoors, so we had to have the lamp lit all day long.

My boyfriend Lesley was a lot older than me and worked in a wood workshop opposite to the school. He had to make coffins. As often as he could, he would meet me from school and walk me back to the cottage. He always seemed to smell of plumber's putty, for that was something else he had to do. Occasionally, I still can smell that. I do not know if maybe he has now passed away. He was my first love; all so sweet and innocent. We were so happy.

I once went to watch him play football in Weymouth with Nan's permission, for she knew by this time and talked to me about the birds and bees, so to speak, and trusted us both. It was a very windy day, and I wore a Nylon jacket, which kept the wind out. When I arrived home, my face wore a beautiful tan, even though it was winter time. There came a time of very great excitement, my 6'6" uncle Tiny, my nan's only remaining son, came home from Stalag 13—prison in Germany, where he had been captured during the war. His real name was Sidney but was always called 'Tiny'.

He was a real, gentle giant and we all loved him. He was in the Grenadier Guards' and had massive holes in his neck, caused by boils whilst in prison as a prisoner of war. The Germans cut the boils out with no anaesthetic and filled holes with salt, if only they realised that was quite a cleanser, or did they? Second night home, all the grownups went to Chequers Inn to celebrate. I can still visualise Nan, all dressed up; green coat, matching hat, black gloves, handbag and shoes; she looked elegant with a handkerchief soaked in Yardley's Lavender.

Uncle Tiny came home to get something and found my brother Ted sitting in Nan's chair, puffing away at her roll-up cigarettes. Uncle just told him how wrong that was and sent him back to bed but did not tell on him to Nan or Granddad—bless him. Poor Nan, she only had four children left out of 13. The only names I can remember of her children were: Uncle Percy, Charlie, Jim, Sid (Tiny), Edith (Amy)—my mum—Queenie, Rose and Winnie. The latter passed at the age of 14 years.

Nan used to make Uncle Tiny drink two raw eggs with vinegar every morning to help build him up as he had lost so much weight. Uncle Tiny always wore a leather belt and Nan would often say to us, "If you do not behave, he will strap you." He would just undo his belt and that was enough for us to behave. Uncle Tiny was such a dear soul, never cruel or unkind.

One day, I had a dreadful fight with cousin Ted because he had beaten my brother Ted up. I tore Ted's fancy pullover and soon, needless to say, Aunt Rose came around to Nan's, being really angry at what I had done. So, Uncle Tiny decided to teach both boys how to box properly so that I would never have to fight my brother's battles again. Brother Ted took up boxing in later years; sadly, I found it really hard to watch him get hurt and shed many tears.

We children learnt so many things that we would never have known about if it had not been for the war, for how many Londoners knew that cows, chickens etc. existed. Whilst with Nan, we only had to attend Sunday school.

Many years later, together with my husband, we returned to Lytchett Matravers to see the old cottage. My goodness, what a change had taken place. The cottage had been extended, rethatched and was beautiful inside and out. There was also a swimming pool in the garden. I knocked on the door and explained that we had been evacuated there. The new owners gladly showed us around, and I was able to tell them exactly where the well was situated. The cottage also had electricity.

Sometime during 1946/1947, we learnt that Mum had finally been allotted a flat in London (St Nicholas Flats, Aldenham St, Euston, NW1). It had three bedrooms, kitchen (very small), bathroom, a very long hall and lounge. The lounge had a window box outside of the window. My Brother Ted planted daffodil bulbs in it and won a prize for doing so. We all returned home to Mum. I was extremely sad, for I missed Nan so very much and, of course, my boyfriend Lesley.

We, first of all, returned to London to a house, being Leighton Rd, Kentish Town before moving to the flat at Euston. Now we did not have to use a tin bath, for there was a proper bathroom and we were now able to take washing to the Kentish Town swimming baths to be washed and dried— called bag wash.

A great excitement came in the form of our dad returning from the war. We also learnt that we had another sister, named Jean, born on the tenth of June 1944. Obviously, Dad was not her dad, as he was still at the time serving his war service out in India.

However, there was a wonderful party held to celebrate Dad's return, but sadly, it turned very sour when Dad tried to strangle our mum because she had given birth to our new sister. It was very frightening for us children. What had really happened was that during the war, our great uncle, who was a cripple, contracted pneumonia and Mum—being the kind person she was—nursed him back to good health. I guess, them being lonely caused the inevitable to happen; that's what war causes besides killing and injuring people.

In time, it was discovered that Dad also had met someone else during the war. It was a very sad and unhappy time for us children and, indeed, for Mum and Dad.

Also at this time, we children were playing outside, when our 7-year-old friend—a boy—saw his daddy coming up the road, dressed in his army uniform. The boy, whose name I cannot recall now, went running down the road to meet his dad, but sadly, a lorry came around the corner and killed our friend. I can still see him in my mind's eye; a lovely boy, with blonde curly hair. We were allowed to see him in his coffin; why, I cannot remember. But I do remember talking to him and telling him that heaven is a beautiful place and his grandma will care for him.

War causes so much pain in so many ways, how I pray that all mankind will come to learn to love one another and live in peace. This was what Mr Winston Churchill also wanted. Now our poor mum had to work to keep her five children and her herself as Dad sent Mum just £5 a month to feed and clothe us all, plus all the other possible needs.

Mum also now had another dog, who was an absolute rascal, into all sorts of mischief, he had to be re-homed because he escaped to the garden next to ours, and destroyed all the chickens.

Kentish Town underground station was a short distance from our home, where we were able to meet mum from her work. In the local area we also had a cinema, so we were able to go to children's matinees. The cinema also had an organ that came up through the floor, whereby we would all sing along to the tunes played by the organist. A swimming pool was also nearby that contained a bathing area, for us to have baths. Also an area where we could wash our laundry and dry it, this was called bag wash.

On the comer of our road was a 'British Restaurant', for this we were given tickets to be able to get very cheap meals.

The Bedford theatre was not very far away in Camden Town, where we paid three pennies to enter what was known as the gods. We often saw Jayne together with her little dog there; Jayne and dog were displayed in the daily papers.

Mum worked in a leather factory, where she made things such as purses, handbags, various broaches and hair bands.

We moved to the flat. I could not settle. I missed my nan so very much. Every day, I watched out of the window, hoping to see her come to see us. Poor Mum had to go to work to keep us all. I remember having to cook breakfast for all my brothers and sisters. The kitchen was so tiny, and on one occasion, the boys were playing around and knocked into me whilst I was carrying a pan full of boiling porridge, and it settled on top of my left foot. Mum took me to the Temperance Hospital, where they treated it for a couple of weeks, but it got no better, so Mum decided to treat it herself with salt, where upon it soon got better.

My two dear brothers, Ted and Terry, were into so much mischief. Our poor mum must have wanted to pull her hair out. They thought that they would be kind to Mum and made toffee, as Mum loved toffee apples. It went wrong, so they emptied it down the sink where, of course, it blocked the pipes. Again out of caring, they tried to unblock the sink by hitting the pipe with an axe. Needless to say, soon those living under our flat became flooded.

Another time, I was home from school due to a headache, when I walked past the large cupboard in the hallway, I heard noises but thought to myself that they were the voices I was accustomed to hearing, talking to me, inside my head. Suddenly, the doors opened and the boys jumped out, really frightening me. They too were wagging from school.

Mum tried to make up for all the work I had to do by hiring a piano teacher, so that I could learn to play music, but alas that did not last for long once Mum discovered that the teacher was wrapping my knuckles with a ruler, in order for me to remember to raise my wrists. Really I did not need the teaching as I could get by listening to a tune and then playing it.

We had an Anderson shelter in the garden, which doubled up as a play room. The top was covered with soil- so once again I was able to create a garden.

Nursing finished, off I went back to school again. Then, my sister, Peggie, caught measles. Silly Pat agreed to sit and read to her. As was usual, she was playing up, and as I said to Mum that I've had it twice so I am safe to sit and read to her. Nurse again, however, I was foolish because I caught it again. This time, it was so bad that I had to go to the Homerton Hospital. Dear me, I was so very ill; delirious most of the time.

When I was ready to go home, much to my mum's annoyance, I was asked to go straight to the White Chapel Hospital, where a doctor explained to Mum and me that they wanted to take a pint of my blood as it could save new born babies whose mothers had contracted measles from going blind. Mum was so cross, as I had lost so much weight. I did not mind at all, for which Mum gave me a kick under the table.

However, the doctor and I won the day, and a pint of blood was taken. I sure hope that it helped the babies. After a little time of convalescence, it was back to school again, ugh. I lost so much schooling, it's a wonder I ever got any.

41

My mum arranged a party for my 14th birthday. All our large family were there. Mum bought me a sky-blue, long-sleeved blouse and a pencil-slim black skirt, plus glasses to put away in a bottom drawer. Also, a 45rpm record of a song called *"Running Bear"*. In later years, 1973 to be exact, I discovered that he was my door keeper and guide during life.

My Grandma was very merry. When she went to the toilet, she kept giggling, then toppled and broke one of my new glasses. I instinctively knew that soon, she would pass to a higher life. The party was held on the 18th December, and Grandma passed away on 5th January due to consumption. Granddad gave me Grandma's engagement ring, which is known as a sleeper or buckle ring. I still have it. Being the eldest of us children, I had to go and see Grandma in the chapel of rest, which I did. Not at all scared, I chatted to her and asked her to give my love to Uncle Jim and other members of the family who had already passed. To me, there is definitely an eternal home, so that was quite natural.

Mum not only went out to work but also did homework, such as sewing by machine such things as the squares on men's shirt sleeves, which she taught me to do also so that I could help her because Mum only received £5 a month to care for us five children, herself, and pay the rent.

My brother, Ted, was a little monkey, always doing things he should not. He wanted to use the sewing machine. I was under strict instructions not to allow children to touch it, but whilst my back was turned, Ted did just that and sewed the needle through his finger. Oh, dear me had to phone Mum at work to take him to the hospital. I was really in trouble for that. It was not easy being the eldest in a family. Nevertheless, I loved them all. At the time of writing this, they have all gone into a greater world before me, i.e. Ted, Terry, Margaret (Peggy) and Jean.

I started work in an office at Oetzmans furniture store, Tottenham Court Road, where I learnt to type, do filing, make tea etc. I loved it there; everyone was kind and friendly. At the end of the first week of working, I was given a packet which enclosed my wages for the week. I did not have a handbag as yet, so I placed the packet in my coat pocket. On the way home, I had to pass Euston Railway Station where I bought some lovely white carnations for Mum and replaced wage packet in my pocket, but alas, when I arrived home, it had gone. My dad was visiting us that weekend. When we told him what happened, sadly, he did not believe me and made me promise that I would repay every penny back, slowly over the weeks ahead, to my mum. That hurt very much; the fact that he disbelieved me, especially as lies are my pet hate.

I became friends with a girl at school, named Kathy. She was a member of a Girls Training Cadets, known as the GTC.

Kathy told my mum all about it. I cannot quite remember what year it was, but I did join the Girls Training Cadets.

Mum suggested it as I was so very shy and a real loner. I used to play bugle in the band and sometimes, beat the big, bass drum, when no one else could be there to do it. I also learnt to lead the band with the mace, tossing and twirling it. We did lots of P.E. and did many different things relating to the horse. I was also very good at doing the Sailor's Hornpipe. I enjoyed all of it, quite a happy time. I used to travel to Kilburn for the GTC nights.

On one occasion, it was so foggy—smog in fact—that I couldn't find the bus stop, which was very scary. We were in GTC, invited to a very large Horse Guards Parade (there were all types of groups, such as Brownies, Girl Guides, Sea Cadets etc.). It was the month of June, a very hot day; 90 degrees, Lady Mountbatten took the salute. Literally, hundreds of girls fainted and made the front page of the newspapers. I didn't faint. Maybe that was because my shirt collar was soaking wet, for which I could thank my mum, for as I was trying to iron my white shirt, but Mum insisted me to prepare the dinner before I left so I had no time to iron it dry.

I was so upset with Mum and pleaded with her to let me iron my shirt dry. Mum got angry and knocked me flying so that I hit my breast against the sideboard; boy, it hurt. But I still got on parade in time. A week or so later, I had a nasty lump come up in my breast; hospital again. This time, they were scared that it was cancer. My poor mum was beside herself, but thank God, the lump was removed and all was well. The only thing was that after the operation, I couldn't pass water so they put my bed by a sink and left a tap dripping. Still to this day, running water has me running quickly to loo.

We also had the honour one year of attending the Royal Albert Hall for the Armistice Parade and Service.

For this, we did a P.E. piece, also the Sailor's Hornpipe, and attended the service, whereby the Poppies fell on our shoulders.

Our uniforms were navy-blue jackets and skirts, white shirt, and black shoes, plus a navy-blue side cap.

Right from a small child, I had always wanted to become a nurse. So, it was. I started my training at the Whittington Hospital Highgate. I enjoyed it, but it was somewhat difficult, time wise. We were paid £1.10 a week, and from that, I had to pay Mum and my bus fares, books, clothing etc. Nevertheless, I continued training and still enjoyed it. There were not many of the original intake left, but those of us that were, were now able to go onto the wards. Firstly, we were inspected by matron; not a hair was allowed to show outside of our nurse's caps, nor were we ever allowed to go out of hospital grounds in our uniforms. Now, we could empty bed pans, fill water jugs, arrange flowers for patients, and make beds, whereby the sheet corners had to be done very precisely in the form of an envelope. I still do that to this day.

One night, I heard banging on my bedroom wall. I discovered that it was Mum. Poor soul; she was in great pain and had a miscarriage of the twins that she was expecting.

It was impossible to go and find a telephone to phone the doctor and help Mum at the same time, so she suggested that I attend to her first. What an experience that was. Mum told me all what to do, and the babies were born. One was completely broken up, the other was absolutely complete and the image of my dad. They were four months old; one boy and one girl. I had to save everything for the doctor to be able to see. To see that dear little baby so complete at 4-months old was to me a complete miracle. I made my mind up there and then that I would never abort a pregnancy.

I eventually managed to go and find a telephone box to be able to phone the doctor and my dad. Mum soon was well and back to work again. Then, Dad went down with malaria, and his condition was so poor that I had to cover him with as many blankets as I could and give him prescribed medicine. The latter was difficult to do as he could not keep still. When Dad was well again, he returned to Colchester where he lived and worked as a chief engineer. It was, when I think back, an odd situation, for Dad would come home once a month to see us children but act as a normal married man, even though he had his lady friend to live with in Colchester. I guess that was real life training in relation to nursing.

Returning to the twin episode, many years later, I was given a message by a medium, all about the twin's episode, and a message from the boy to say that he would always protect me. That to me was a proof that there is a life after this life. Whilst at Oetzmans, I became friendly with a family of three people; Albert, who worked in a place that prepared goods for delivery, his brother-in-law Robert, who was a driver, and Albert's sister called Laura. They lived with their wheel chair bound mother at the Archway, Kentish Town.

Laura did all the dusting at the firm. We became friends because Albert came to my office one day and asked me if I could type a letter for him. Someone had advertised for someone who would give a good home for an Airedale dog. He knew how I loved dogs, and he too had a passion for Airedales. Of course, I did that for him, and they became the owners of this special animal. He was so grateful that I was invited to meet the Airedale. I had a crush on Albert who was double my age, but I guess in a way, he was like a father to me. He also was, as I realised many years later, a loner because really, he was gay. I used to be invited to all the family weddings etc.

Whilst still working at Oetzmans, I became very friendly with a young man called John, and he wanted me to marry him. His mother said that we could have the top half of her house and turn it into a flat. We worked hard, decorating it and making curtains etc. Then one day, I became aware that we were not as suited as I had hoped and knew beyond a shadow of doubt that we were not meant to be anything other than friends. So, I broke off our engagement.

But John would not take no for an answer, so to get away from him, I did a second job as usherette at the Gaumont Cinema, but alas, even that did not keep him at bay. So, I told Albert all about it and asked him if he could pretend to be my boyfriend, meet me after cinema and talk to John.

Albert, being a wise man, recommended a work friend, who was young like me and apparently also had designs towards me, though I didn't realise this at the time. His name was Arthur. He met me after cinema duty, as did John, and we went to a café where I consumed 16 cups of coffee whilst trying to make John understand that at this stage in my life, I did not feel ready to become a wife. There was still so much more I would like to do. I took pains to try and make him understand that I had allowed all the preparations to continue simply because I did not know how to tell him how I truly felt for fear of hurting him. I was really very very sorry. It was really very sad for him, my mum and me. Of course, for his mum too.

****

Except for Christmas cards, Albert and I kind of lost touch from 1968. Until one day in 1983, when suddenly he became very strongly into my thoughts, so I plucked up courage and telephoned him. His sister answered the telephone and said, "Pat, I am sorry to say that I doubt he will be able to come to the phone as he is very ill with cancer." However, he did come to the phone to speak to me and was thrilled that I had phoned. He explained how ill he was and that he felt that his time was near to pass, "Please, will you pray for me?"

"Of course," I said, "I will, and I hope you will soon be free from the pain and have a safe journey into your new life free from all the pain, and thanks for always being my friend." He passed to a higher life the very next day. Since then, I have received many messages from him via many different mediums.

****

We left café, and Arthur took me home and made a date with me to go to cinema the next evening to see *Street Car Named Desire* but alas, during the film, I became ill; my neck and head hurt me terribly. I just felt so very ill, so he kindly took me home. Mum—bless her—thought that I was pulling the lead, so to speak, as she was so cross that I had broken up with John. Mum had made all the dresses for our wedding. I went to bed and apparently my aunt Ginny came to see my mum. When Mum told her that I was presumably ill, Aunt Ginny asked to see me. There and then she realised that I was truly very ill; she became known as my fairy-god mother after that (In later life, if I am tempted to drink coffee, I get an aura migraine).

I was unable to keep my head still and kept moving it from left to right continuously. Aunt was very worried, so trotted off to Euston Station and brought a doctor home. He immediately called an ambulance and I was transferred to the hospital, whereupon it was discovered that I had polio and meningitis. Apparently, our home had to be fumigated. I was ill for a very long time.

On one occasion, when I awoke having lost conscientiousness, I thought that I was in my own coffin, for all around my bed, there were tables of flowers (my aunt was a florist). There was also a lady sitting by my bed, all dressed in black that I recognised as a nun. When I mentioned it to the nurse, she said that there was no one there. Many years later, when meditating, I discovered that the Nun was a Mother Superior, who was my guardian angel.

I cannot remember how long I was in the hospital, but when I came out, I was unable to walk, and doctors had said that I would never be able to walk again or even have children (Many years later, I gave birth to three children with intervals of 5 years and 7 years). The doctors did not know what wonderful brothers I had; they encouraged me in every way possible, and eventually, they caused me to walk, even took me to Regents Park where they rode bicycles and I had to walk beside them and, much later, run beside them. That was all very hard work but was a great success; I can never thank my brothers enough.

In time, I was able to re-start work but not my nursing training. This time, I worked at the Middlesex Hospital, Mortimer St. in the X-ray department, entering appointments, filing etc. My friend Arthur joined the army as a grenadier guardsman and in later years, passed away due to a T.B. condition. That was a painful loss for me and of course, a painful loss for his family.

By the time I was 18 and a half years, I decided that I wanted to join the WRAF. Mum was away on holiday at that time. I knew that Mum would not like me to join up, so I went to Colchester to see my dad and got him to sign his permission for me to do so. He suggested that I should join all the sports programmes that I could; this I did.

Mum was very upset when she returned from holiday, but in the end, gave me her blessing. Mind you, I had been a little crafty to get her blessing, for whilst she was away, I re-decorated her kitchen. When painting the door, I decided to paint it with two different colours, which did not bode well with my dear Mum; she was very cross indeed. I felt quite hurt after that; especially so, as when I tried to get the lid off of tin, which was a tin that previously held baby milk food and was dented, I badly cut the top of my little finger, for which I had to attend hospital. I must have been a real pain in the butt to my lovely Mum.

My mum—bless her—gave me a talk about the birds and the bees, so to speak, and how to look after myself and never to accept a cigarette if offered, in case it was a drug. (Mum herself had been a chain smoker and had suffered from tobacco poisoning, whereby she was in hospital and almost lost her life.)

So, Mum had prepared me to set out into the wide world as safely as she was able to do.

However, Mum, together with my sisters, saw me off at Euston Station to Wilmslow, Manchester (my two dear brothers by this time were in Royal Navy training). I surprised myself at the station, for I did not get at all upset but Mum and sisters did. I did eight weeks training.

One of the very first items to do was collect bedding from the stores. Lo and behold, the airman in charge of this offered me an American cigarette. Remembering what Mum had told me, I politely refused. We then had lots of marching, making sure that we were all in step, followed by bull, which is cleaning one's place of living and getting uniforms fitted, and name labels sewn on to every garment.

Then we had exams and tests, in order to discover what type of trade we were capable of doing. Plus, many different injections were injected to protect us from various illnesses, and each lot of injections caused me to be hospitalised; they obviously did not suit me. After four weeks, we were given a weekend pass to go home. This time when I returned to camp, whilst having breakfast, I really did miss home and was very upset. Apparently, I was in line to be a top cadet but lost it because I would not tell on a friend regarding something she said to a NAAFI person; that's life.

I had leave, after which I was transferred to R.A.F. Waddington, bomber command where I worked in the control tower and sometimes in the operations room. My title was 'operations clerk'. I enjoyed it. My very first day working in control tower was somewhat strange. One had to write down every word heard on the R.T.

An aircraft had crashed into the sea. Bodies were floating on the water and that made me feel very sad. Another lass, named Gamy, advised me to have one of her cigarettes, a Woodbine (I thought that one would be okay). From that day on, I also smoked. A year or so later, I answered a call on R.T. from a certain call sign. As the controller had a reason to leave the room, the pilot calling was the duke of Edinburgh, and when the controller returned, he took over again, and much to both our surprises, the duke asked for the angel he had already spoken to, to be able to continue to talk to him. Needless to say, that was not allowed.

I joined all the sports that I could. I played cricket whereby we visited many other R.A.F. stations. We used to go by coach and on our return journey, had wonderful sing songs. On one occasion, Gamy shouted at the driver to stop immediately. She got off the coach and ran into a field, where she found a sheep on its back and managed to turn it over and back onto its feet. If she had not done that, it could have died.

There came a time when I received a phone call from Mum to say that Nan was very ill and not expected to live very long and if it was possible that we could go together to see her. She was now in a hospital in Bournemouth. I managed to get a three-day pass. I had very little money, so I decided to try and hitchhike to London from Waddington, Lincs. I was very lucky that a very kind driver, who was a family man, gave me a lift and arranged for another driver to meet me and return me to camp.

Mum and I caught the Bournemouth Belle train and duly went to the hospital to see Nan. Bless her, she had had a stroke. She looked very pretty as the nurses had cut her hair into a bob in order to relieve the pressure on her head. Sadly, she was completely paralyzed. Eventually, she went to stay with her daughter, my aunt Queenie, still totally paralysed, and was so for another 18 months after which she passed to her eternal home of the spirit.

Mum and I returned to London, where this new driver took me on to Lincoln, but oh dear, he was not so kind as the first one. All was okay for a few miles, then he started to touch my knee and tried to hold hands. I did my best to keep my cool and hoped for a situation where I could make an escape. At one stage, he stopped the lorry and said that he was going to have a sleep, after which we could have a cuddle. I was very worried, so when I heard him snoring, out I got and ran and ended up walking from Grantham to Waddington; it was a very long way. I felt exhausted, but thank God, I was safe and needless to say, I never ever hitchhiked again.

Few months after Nan passed away, several other girls and I were doing night duty in the operations room. There was no flying taking place due to weather conditions, when one of them suggested that we make and play on an Ouija Board i.e. a board with letters of the alphabets around in a circle, plus two words: yes and no, and an upturned glass that one placed one's fingers on lightly.

I had never known of such a thing, but I was persuaded that it was all okay to do, so I joined in. One of the girls said a little prayer. No one but me received anything. The glass moved to the letters, spelling out "for Pat, from her nan, Baker: I am fine x." That certainly was my nan's surname before she married Ted.

The girls asked if I did have a Nan who had died. They were as surprised as I was but grateful. The strange thing was that when we went to unlock the very thick and wide door, which was definitely locked before we started duty there, it was found to be unlocked. We could have been in a lot of trouble for that, and it was not our doing. Of course, in later years, I learnt that it was unwise to play with such things as 'Ouija boards' as a lot of mischief could be caused.

Writing about Nan has reminded me of something regarding my nan. After she had passed away, if ever there was something that was not so good going to happen in our family, I would dream of her. She would in the dream be, dressed in her wedding dress but in her coffin. This happened when I was home on leave once. We were awaiting my brother Ted to come on leave, whereby we hoped to celebrate his 21st birthday.

In the dream, Nan told me that Ted would not be home as he had a slight accident, and an officer would be calling to tell Mum all about it. Wow, dear me, should I tell my mum? Eventually, I plucked up courage and did so. Mum was so upset and said, "You are a very wicked girl to say something like that. I pray that you never have any dreams of that sort again." Lo and behold, a short time later, a knock at our door brought the officer that my nan had spoken of, and yes, Ted had an accident which caused him to lose the tops of his fingers.

Mum rushed off to Portsmouth Naval Hospital. Ted and others were unloading ammunition. He had called to his oppo to hold on for a while, but the lad still continued, and hence, Ted's fingers were trapped. Once leave was finished, I returned to my station. We used to have a NAAFI on camp; not many of us liked it, so we used to go to Sally Ann instead, which was run by the Salvation Army. They had comfortable arm chairs, lots of nice goodies to eat, a good cup of tea and always someone willing to chat to you. I learnt how to use and fire a rifle and got quite good at it. I never ever intended to use one for killing anything, but it was useful at a fairground firing range, where I won lots of prizes.

Besides cricket, I took up running and hurdling. Alas, on one occasion, a sergeant suggested that I place my right leg over the hurdle first and not as I was doing left leg over the hurdle. What a fool I was in doing as she suggested, for I fell and damaged my right ankle. It was a weekend and the medical officer was not on duty. For the whole weekend, I was in terrible pain. On Monday, the MO saw it. Dear me, it was so swollen up, like a balloon that they sent me off in an ambulance to a R.A.F. hospital where the leg was put into plaster of Paris from knee to toes. I was told that I had damaged ligaments and cracked a bone.

During this time, I received a letter from the officer in charge of the GTC to say that they were allotted a certain amount of tickets to be able to attend the queen's coronation. A raffle had taken place and my name was also entered. Guess what? I had won a seat for the coronation. I managed to get a leave, and off I went. My seat was opposite to Horse Guards Parade. Sadly, it rained and my plaster got wet.

Thankfully, a kind policeman arranged for a police car to take me to the hospital, where it was all sorted out, but I missed most of the very exciting day and was able to join the celebrations that evening that were held on the street where my mother lived. That was 1953.

It went on for months: plaster off, new one on, and then strapping replaced plaster; all to no avail, I was still in pain. I was sure the powers that be thought that I was making it all up. However, I was sent back to the hospital and still, they could not find what was wrong with the ankle. One day, I was awaiting transport to return to my station when a wing commander visited the ward to see other patients. He was a surgeon, attached to the R.A.F.

Many of the patients had requested me to go to NAAFI to buy their goodies. It was getting close to the time that they closed, so there was I, creeping out of the ward when this loud voice commanded me to stop; it was the wing commander calling me. He asked me what was wrong with the leg, and I told him what had happened and that no one seemed to know why I was still in pain. He requested that I return to my bed and that he would take a look at it in time, which he did, saying that he thought that I had torn the ligament that would never heal without an operation.

He explained what he was going to do and told me that I would be bedridden for so many weeks and that I would be in plaster from my big toe right up to very top of the leg. If I was happy to trust him, I would have to sign a form for him to go ahead in a week's time.

I agreed and the operation took place. When I came around from operation, I was in terrible pain. Dearie me, I so wanted my mum, but alas, I had never told her. She was still paying back the money that she had borrowed in order for us to go to Nan's funeral. She did not need any further expense by coming to see me, which she would have done if I had told her.

I used to get visitors of other patients to post letters to her well outside of the hospital. Where ever I needed to go, I was transported to on stretcher trolley, even to hospital cinema. From the time of fall to being complete again took 18 months. But I thank God with all my heart for that really helpful wing commander. I had a leave to go home, needless to say, Mum was cross that I had not told her but she understood my reasons.

When I returned to camp, I found that I had been posted to a new station: R.A.F. Wittering, near Stamford, Lincolnshire, still as an operations clerk in the control tower. It was a smaller station, a little bit closer to London. I was quite happy there. Gamy, my friend, was also there, so that made life a lot happier. I met my husband-to-be there. He was a fireman, so he was mostly stationed outside of the control tower.

I thoroughly enjoyed my time in W.R.A.F. I had one very special friend called Anne Game, known affectionately as Gamie. She was quite a vivacious person, always such fun to be with. She and I were bridesmaids to another lass, who married a R.A.F. chap. Actually, Gamie and I wore bridesmaids' dresses that my mum had made for my cancelled wedding, and the bride wore the dress that Mum had made for me, so that pleased her to think that they were able to be used. I cannot recall the bride's name, but I think that it was Rosie. We were surprised at the reception, held in bride's home, because the groom disappeared to see a football match. I guess it was a marriage of convenience due to her expecting a baby.

How sad for them both. I don't know what happened to Rosie as we all left Waddington due to repairs etc. being done and moved to Wittering, near Peterborough, where the nearest town was Stamford.

At R.A.F. Wittering, our hours on duty were changed. We seemed to be doing many more hours on duty to what we had been used to at R.A.F. Waddington. This made life so much more difficult for us all as now we were doing 12 hours of duty and 12 hours off. In that time off, of course, there should have been eight-hour sleep and four hours to fit in courses, washing, ironing, cleaning etc., plus any personal shopping we needed and, of course, courting. A time came when I slept for two days and missed one of my classes, no excuses, and jankers for you my gal, and peeling potatoes for 3 days.

I guess these extra hours, plus my husband-to-be and I courting, made my body think that enough is enough. Now, I had boils in my ear drums. I was back to sick quarters, where the powers had to send an aircraft to Scotland to obtain the drugs required to clear the problem up. After 14 days, I was back on duties.

Whilst working in the control tower, when we made tea/coffee, sometimes the firemen would come up for tea, one of which was to become my husband.

We were courting for approximately 18 months and during that time, we got engaged and Mum arranged an engagement party for us. That was great, but I was not used to drinking. At that time, I was drinking Port (I was not accustomed to any kind of drink at that stage); however, I became very tired and simply just wanted to go to bed and sleep. Mum thought otherwise. She believed that it was much too early for me to retire and insisted that I stayed up and had another drink. Oh dear, that turned out to be a very unwise decision, for I apparently became abusive and said some very unkind things to my mum.

The next day, Mum was not talking to me and no one would tell me what it was I had said to her. No matter how hard I tried, not one single person would tell me.

Of course, I apologised but all Mum would say is "a drunken man/woman apparently always speaks the truth."

To this day, I still do not know, though I suspect it was something to do with us being sent away during the war, as I know I did resent that. That is just my surmise, maybe one day, when we meet in the great beyond, I may find out. I hate to think that I hurt my mum, for I loved her dearly and always will. Of course, I know now that our parents did what they thought was wisest for our safety.

Anyhow, we soon made up and Mum started planning the wedding.

Ron and I married on the 31st July, 1954, at St Mary's Church, Eversholt St, Euston, St Pancras area of London. Mum made the bridal dress, plus ten bridesmaids and two page boys. It seemed that every time I went home for w/e leave, she had yet another bridesmaid for me. There were two of each colour in the rainbow.

Norman, a friend of me and my brother in the R.A.F., was Ron's best man and became friends with Ron's Sister, Joan, who was a bridesmaid and they later got married. My dad gave me away. My lovely brothers were there too.

That rainbow has always had a special place in my heart, as Mum used to sing '*Somewhere over the Rainbow*' to us children. Mum must have worked her socks off to do all that for me and my future husband.

We went on honeymoon to my aunts Rose's and Queenie with one shilling in old money, which is now worth 10 p. Can you just imagine that? Thank God to aunts for we did manage to go to Bournemouth, also Sandbanks and Shell Bay, which was lovely except for the fact that Ron, being very fair skinned, got very sun burnt. I bathed him with cool milk, and he was fine the next day.

The reason that we went on honeymoon with only one shilling was that we had decided that I would pay for the main event and Ron was arranging for the honeymoon. When I questioned where it was we were going on honeymoon, Ron just said: "Wait and see. I have pigs at home which Mum and Dad are selling for me, and it depends on how much they sell for, but I promise it will be very good."

Wow! A day after wedding, I said, "Well, where is it we are going? Where is the lovely surprise?"

It was then that he revealed that he had no such thing as pigs for sale and his parents knew nothing of it. Quite laughable now, the term 'pigs might fly' comes to mind and it turned out to be the first of many fibs to come.

It was all so very upsetting and embarrassing, but both sets of parents and my aunts all helped to calm things down and suggested that we went to stay with Aunt Rose, and between them all, they paid for the taxi and train fares, plus providing our food for a week. What a family to have!

My aunts lived in Dorset.

After honeymoon, it was back to R.A.F. Wittering, where we rented a Caravan on the edge of a runway. My God, it was bitter cold; sometimes, we had to sleep with our overcoats on the bed.

Patricia as an evacuee in Wales

Patricia in the Girls Training Corps

Patricia in the WRAF

Crowds await HMS Hermes

HMS Hermes returning from the Falklands War

Prince Philip at RAF Waddington greeting the crew of the Canberra which won an air race in 1953.

Saint Theresa of Roses

Patricia's lovely dog, 'Shep'

A healing hand for the world

HOUR in the company of ialist healer Pat Pizzey is an ing experience that provides food for thought.

effectively picked up the torch was lit by Edna Wardle, the found-sident of Horley Spiritualist Church l in London Road.

e are Saturday and Sunday services as healing days on Mondays and sdays. Pat also gives talks at other list churches.

s first spiritual experience occurred the war when she was evacuated entish Town, London.

as only five years old at the time iad to leave behind a dog which I learly, named Bobby. I found I ee him clearly in a circle of light. I 1 every night.

rote to my mother to ask if he was at and she said nothing had hap-o him.

when I went back to London nine years later, mother had to tell me the truth.

"The air raid siren had gone and she had run out of the house. Then she realised that she had forgotten her handbag and Bobby ran back in to get it. But the house was hit and the door lintel came down on Bobby's back. He died there and then," said Pat.

Experiences

At that young age Pat didn't realise she had had spiritual experiences.

During her evacuation she had stayed with her grandmother who told her of a remarkable event.

"She had lost her husband one day, and a daughter the following day. But when she was giving birth to another baby she says she saw her husband and daughter standing on either side of her," said Pat.

Her own confinement provided Pat with her most remarkable spiritual experience.

"A few years later, just after I had given birth to my youngest son I died for a very short time.

"I went into the spirit world and I saw my mother. Now my mother would never wear anything green when she was alive, but she was wearing the most beau-tiful pale green dress — there are no words to describe it, the colour I could see were unbeliev-able, and there was a feeling of absolute, perfect love all around.

"I said, 'Mum I would love to stay with you here, but who would look after the baby?' and immediately I regained my life," said Pat.

"People may ridicule you as much as they like, but I have seen what I have seen, and I have been left with no fear of dying."

Another remarkable story revolves around a drawing made by a psychic artist. It was given to a woman who was told that it was not for her but for a woman who would come to see her in three days time — that was Pat.

"She gave me this rolled up piece of paper with a rib-bon round it — I unrolled it and I couldn't believe my eyes. It was a perfect draw-

HEALING AND HELP: Pat Pizzey of the Horley Spiritualist Church, founded by Edna Wardle seen in the painting. Picture: GAVIN HODGE

'I went into the spirit world and I saw my mother'

ing of my grandmother," said Pat.

When first she came to Horley Spiritualist Church she said she was shy and sat in the back row.

"Nobody there knew me because I had only recently come up from London. But Miss Wardle came straight up to me. I went beetroot red, but she described my mother to me, and she told me I had a red purse which had belonged to my mother. It was locked away in a tin which was locked in a cupboard, she said. She also told me there was a half-crown in it and she told me the date on the coin.

"I remembered the purse then, and we looked it out when we got home — the date on the coin was right, too," said Pat.

From that day on Pat became more involved with the church and the healings. She broke her ankle and healing sessions helped her get fit again quickly.

"I saw people a lot worse than I was and wished I could do something for them. I was asked to join the healing team," said Pat.

Pat and her husband, Bob, live in a Horley Manse, a bungalow behind Horley Church, and two years hard work — helped by friends — has produced a truly beautiful garden at the back.

Pat says the Horley Spiritualist Association is not affiliated to any organisation, religious or otherwise, but does believe in the Fatherhood of God and the continuous exis-tence of the human soul.

Anyone is welcome at the services which are held at 7.30pm on Saturdays and 6.30pm on Sundays at Hor-ley Church in the out-of-town section of London Road, opposite Chantry Park.

A news article about Patricia

Horley Spiritualist Church

Patricia pictured recently

I left the W.R.A.F. in April 1955 as I was expecting our first baby. It was quite a wrench, leaving husband at Wittering.

My mother-in-law had said that we could live with her until we could get a place of our own. Neither of us had thought things out very carefully, such as to where the baby's cot would go, for we were sleeping, when Ron was on leave, in a tiny-box room with a single bed (Nice and cosy though).

Then, Ron had not told me that when children started work, the custom was that the mother took their wages and handed back to them what she considered was sufficient for their needs.

Now, it was the same in my case too. My mother-in-law would go with me when I visited the post office to collect my allowance, take the money and give me back what she thought was enough for me to live on. This, indeed, made it very difficult to prepare for our baby.

I was completely at a loss to know what I could do about the baby's clothes, nappies, cot, pram etc. There was no animosity towards my mother-in-law and we got on very well, but her law had to be followed and that was that. However, on one occasion when my allowance was due, mother-in-law was ill and unable to go with me to the post office. Hence, I plucked up courage and hopped on a train to London to see my mum and asked her advice. I sent a telegram to mother-in-law to say that I had gone to London to see my mum.

My mum told me in no uncertain terms that I had to find somewhere for us to live as soon as possible. "You have made your bed, gal, now you must lie in it. Have a rest for a few days, then start searching for a home to rent."

Wow, that was a blow. So, I tramped the streets for three weeks and finally, found one room at the top of a Victorian house, right opposite Holloway Prison. We had to share the kitchen with all the other people in the house—not an easy task at all—and to crown it all, it was at the time that Ruth Ellis was hung in Holloway Prison; she was the last woman to be hung for a crime.

The whole road was packed with people. I just couldn't stay there so I walked all the way to Mum's home in Euston as buses couldn't get through the road. I was approximately eight months with a child at that time; a very hot day too. Shortly after that, my husband came out of the R.A.F. and got work as a driver. On the 15 July, 1955, our first child was born, during a real old thunderstorm; mind you, it was St Swithin's Day.

Tina Patricia Rose was christened in the hospital, as she was very small and quite weak at first. Sadly, she cried day and night and her daddy didn't have much patience. Of course with driving, he needed his sleep but with all of us in one room, there was nowhere I could take her for him to get his sleep. It was also frightening as mice could be heard each night, and I found one in her cot once. This made me keep the light on during most nights.

I was exhausted looking after Tina, she was always crying, and no matter what I told the doctors, they all said that I was a fussy, worried mother and there was nothing wrong with her, but I always felt that there was something wrong, but they would not listen. One day, the landlady of the house offered for me to put Tina in her pram and place the pram in the garden. She would watch over her so that I could have a well-deserved sleep which I did, but alas, I woke up suddenly and instinctively knew that something was wrong with my baby.

I flew down the stairs to find that Tina had turned onto her tummy and her lips were blue. I picked her up and rubbed her back until life seemed to come back into her. Needless to say, I never left her with anyone again. It was a very traumatic time as her father had no patience whatsoever and was always threatening to kill her. Even when doctors said I was to leave her to cry, I just dared not to in case he harmed her.

Tina was baptised in the hospital as she was so tiny.

The day that we were able to go home from the hospital, my dad came to Mum's, especially to see his first grandchild, but he didn't tell us that he was supposed to be at Liverpool St Station to meet his woman (Pat, for they were then going off on holiday). He was so pleased to see his granddaughter and stayed longer than he should have.

Next thing: Pat was at Mum's door. She came in and made a real fuss about being left at the station. There was such a ding dong going on that the shock caused me to lose the milk I should have been breast feeding my baby with, but what did surprise me was that my mum was so understanding towards Pat.

So, poor Tina now had to be bottle fed, which in itself was a nightmare. As soon as she was fed, it would come gushing back. "Nothing is wrong," said the doctors, "she is just a difficult child."

But how wrong they were, for when she was about 13–14 years old, she had appendicitis. Her operation took hours, as her appendix was attached to her intestines, hence the difficulty in feeding.

The day may come when doctors will listen to a mother's intuition.

Life was very hard living in the one room and sharing the kitchen with all the others in the house. Nappies had to be boiled in a bucket on top of the gas cooker. There were only a gas cooker and a sink in the kitchen. It was also very difficult to live on just one wage packet coming in. Driving jobs did not pay great sums of money. So, bless her, Mum said that she would look after Tina if I would like to try and find work. So, this I did and worked in an office at Gilbeys, the wine merchants.

I learnt two very good lessons there. One was that for an upset tummy, one should take one measure of brandy, plus one measure of port and results: tummy all better in no time. The other was that my Sister Peggy wanted a job. Would I speak for her at Gilbeys? Mum—bless her—advised me not to. She said that it never works out, "You will find that you will have to leave." But silly Pat, I felt sorry for my sister, and she joined me at Gilbeys. During this time, my so loved granddad had a fall whilst cleaning the windows of his bedroom.

They were the type one saw in old Victorian houses. He had a very large Victorian wardrobe. He slipped on steps whilst cleaning the windows, grabbed onto the wardrobe, and fell with the wardrobe on top of him. Poor man, he broke his leg quite badly and had to stay in the hospital. The fall caused cancer. Doctors wanted to operate, but he refused. Mum and Dad came to see me and explained that he needed this operation but wouldn't listen to anyone. They assured me that he would listen to me and if I could see him and ask him to have the same. This I did reluctantly, and he agreed to have the operation. But sadly, he died whilst having the operation. It took me years to get over that. I felt that it was entirely my fault, and I loved him so much. He was my dad's father.

Sadly, through Granddad's passing, my dad arranged for my husband, Tina and I to have his ground-floor flat in the Victorian house, 10 Ampthill Sq. N.W.1. London. It consisted of two rooms, one large bedroom and a large room which was kitchen and dining area. In the basement was a really dirty old place which held a brick boiler in one corner where I could really boil the washing properly. I had to light a fire under the copper boiler. It was marvellous to have more than one room, plus a little garden that backed onto Euston Railway Station. That was not so good for the washing, so I had to dry it indoors. We had an outside toilet there.

I had a problem with mice there too but was advised to crush some glass and put in mouse holes. Apparently, if they cut themselves, they then ran away. Well, it worked, I hated to think of them cut though, but it was better than trapping them in a trap. Life was tough living there, as a lady who lived above us was always threatening to tell authorities who owned the property that we were there, Dad didn't tell us we should not have been there, and of course, Tina still cried, which upset the dear lady.

On top of that, Gilbeys were laying off staff (no redundancy pay in those days). Yes, Mum was right; Peggy was okay, but Pat was out. However, I managed to get a better job as an internal audit clerk at N.U.A.W. Grays Inn Road. I quite enjoyed it there and all the girls got on well together.

Sandra (Sandy) was one of the lasses that worked there. She was a lovely person, but sadly, she was very ill and taken to the hospital.

I met her mum one day at the bus stop. She told me that Sandra was very delirious and had told her mum that she had been riding on a beautiful, white horse, so I guessed that somehow she was going to pass. Lo and behold, she did the next day, which should have been her wedding day, and she was buried on what would have been her 18th birthday.

It was another very sad time. She was such a beautiful girl in all kinds of ways and had lovely, long, ginger hair. Many years later, I received from a psychic artist a drawing of Sandra. And later still had a message from a medium as to her passing away on her wedding day and being buried in her wedding dress on her birthday. (How is that, as to prove that life continues after death?)

Whilst still working there, I was delighted to find that I was expecting again, 1959/60. We also managed to get a one-bedroom flat in St Nicholas Flats, Aldenham St., Euston. Same block as Mum lived in. It was on top floor, so it had lots of stairs to bump pushchair up and down. Now, we had a bedroom, a lounge, a kitchen, and a proper bathroom; marvellous. Kitchen was large enough to have our meals in. At last, we were able to have a washing machine also.

I worked until the end of April 1960. Then one morning on 23rd June, I woke up at 4:45 am and knew that my new baby was on the way; off to hospital, Highgate London. Anthony David Ronald was born at 6:45 am. I was so excited. It was a boy, which I so wanted. I checked to make sure that all his fingers and toes were in place and was so surprised to notice that he looked the image of Great Aunt Annie Davey. He weighed in at 7lbs 1oz. He was a lovely baby, but sadly, he got yellow jaundice and had to be put in an incubator for a while. His second Christian name was given to him after the great singer David Whitfield. My mum was so thrilled to have a grandson,

She looked after Tina whilst I was in the hospital. Apparently, Tina offered to sell her brother to her nan for half a crown, i.e. 2s 6p.

Sadly, it took Tina a long while to accept her brother, for there was a difference of 5 years between them. She did eventually. We couldn't afford for me to be able to stay at home as a proper Mum should, so Mum kindly looked after both Tina and Tony. Of course, I paid her, and there couldn't be anyone better than their nan to look after them. And I returned to National Union of Agricultural Workers as internal audit clerk. But that wasn't to be for long, as several of us girls applied for a male person's position after he had left, but as was usual in those days, another male was brought in from outside. So, quite a few of us left. I managed to get an even better job as a clerical supervisor at C and A Modes, Surveyors Dept, Marble Arch. I loved it, but there was such a lot of catching up to be done with correspondence and letters were months behind. Then there was the whole costing for the new branch in Edinburgh. I was foolish enough to take work home with me to bring it all up to date. Which I did; I really loved my work.

Life, as a whole was quite pleasant. Money, from both of us working, enabled us to go on holidays and to hire a car when visiting my husband's parents in Eastwood, Notts. We always spent one Christmas with my mum and the next with his, and on Easter we would visit his parents also. When we went on holiday, Mum would come too. Sadly, my husband would always be accusing me of going out with other men. My God, I never ever had the chance to do such a thing, nor would I have ever thought of doing so. Mum used to say,

"Well dear, don't you think that it's possible when he accuses you, it's really him doing so?"

"No," I used to say, "he wouldn't do that." Silly lass that I was, eh because that's exactly what he was doing, and Mum and sisters all knew but couldn't tell me. Before I could say boo to a goose, he left and went back to his mother's to be with his girlfriend. The children were, like me, devastated, so after a while, my mum persuaded me to take them up to Nott's to see him and try and reconcile. He agreed and said that he would sort things out with his girlfriend and then come back.

He eventually came for a weekend, and actually for the first time ever, he took me out for a meal, and yes, he came back a fortnight later. We all settled down nicely again, then one day, a knock came at the door, and lo and behold, it was the girlfriend. I remembered how kind my mum was to Dad's girlfriend, so I invited her in to wait for Ron, who was coming home from work.

She begged me to let him go back to her as she loved him dearly, the fact that he had two dear children didn't seem to matter to her. She wanted him and that was that. However, he told her that he couldn't leave again and eventually, saw her back to the railway station, swearing that it was all over. But a month later, I guess it took that time to give his notice in. He was off again to her, or so I thought, but his mum said that it was someone else this time.

Off we went again to Notts, and his parents advised him to return to his family, whereupon we all settled down again. But he was somewhat restless and begged me to move with him to Australia, but there was no way I could leave my mum and family or even his. He said that he hated London. So, I promised that if anything ever happened to my mum, then I would at least move to the country side for his sake, and it would probably be better for the children.

Well, 1966; wow, what a year that was. We—Ron, myself, Tina and Tony, and my mum and Dad too came from Colchester—went to Jersey for a holiday that was at the time of the World Cup for football, which England won. I can remember my mum being so cross that Dad wanted to watch the match; mind you, I must admit that I wanted to watch it too; it was so exciting.

We had a lovely holiday. Mum, other than the football game time, was so very happy. The time for the holiday came around so quickly that we didn't have sufficient cash in time, so we had to borrow £200 from my dad. Ron promised faithfully to pay him back but he never did, so I repaid Dad £100.

In August, there was the Aberfan disaster, where many children were buried alive at school, when a coal slick due to wet weather slid down on top of their school that was absolutely dreadful. All hearts went out to their parents and families.

Then on 23rd August, 1966, we had our own disaster. We were then living in a flat in Albany Street, behind the old Bedford Theatre, Camden Town. I got up for work that morning, but for some unknown reason, I just could not rush like I normally did. I took the children half way to my mum's and then went to the bus stop to go to Marble Arch.

Whilst waiting for the bus, Mum's neighbour's daughter came up to me and said, "I think you should go back to your mum's as police are there."

I replied, for instinctively I knew, "You mean, my mum has died?"

"I don't know," she said. So, I set off for Mum's home.

Two policemen were there. They asked me to sit down and told me that my mum had died. They advised me not to go into lounge to see her, but I said that I must; that's my mum, which I did and then got a bowl of water and washed her feet. Why I did that, I really did not know (was it some kind of thought that that is what Jesus did for his disciples; I really do not know). The police must have thought that I was mad.

I went to Mum's neighbour's house, who kindly let me use the phone, and I phoned my dad at Paxman's of Colchester, where he was a chief engineer. He arranged to come up as soon as possible. Then, the police kindly took me to my brother Ted's home to tell him and my sisters Peg and Jean. I can't remember how I got in touch with my brother Terry, who lived in Havant, Hants.

Strange thing is though I had suspected for about a year that my mum would pass over to a higher life, what made me think that was Mum hated the colour green. I once bought her a beautiful green dress, but she would never wear it. But strange thing was that she had bought and put up some of the prettiest green tiles, and put them up behind her cooker (Mum was quite a do-it-yourself enthusiast; always buying the latest tools etc.).

When I saw them, I instinctively knew that my mum would not be here for long, but as one does, one dismisses the thought, hoping that it will not come true. (I guess, there's a lesson there: to never dismiss those thoughts that come into one's mind.) I recall that the evening before Mum passed away, I called to see her. When I was ready to leave, Mum came out of the door and waved to me until she could no longer see me.

The day after Mum passed away, I went around to Mum's home to see Dad and to discuss funeral arrangements etc. to find Dad standing on the balcony, crying. I had never seen him cry before; however, he said, "Come in, I've some sad news to tell you." What a shock it was to be told that my sister Jean's husband, who was 24 years of age, had died from a heart attack in the early hours of 24th August, 1966. My poor sister had now lost her mum and husband within 24 hours. All our lives were shattered.

Poor Jean, she had three children at that time. As is the way that I am, when I'm troubled, I throw myself into as much hard work as I can, and I set to cleaning everything in my mum's flat, ready for her to be brought home after the autopsy. Every day, my brother Ted would polish her coffin, and I would tend to her make up.

We all had many discussions as to whether the children, Tina and Tony, should go to the funeral; after all, they were the ones who found Mum. But everyone, except for me, thought that they should not, so I accepted the majority decision. (Many years later, my son Tony informed me that he would never forgive me for not letting him go to his nan's funeral.) Of course, I can see now that the children should have gone. We had a double funeral for Mum and Dave; there seemed to be miles of cars following.

On the same balcony as my mum lived, was a lady who was mentally retarded, who could be very fierce and used to beat her own mother up. This dear soul took a lot of Mum's flowers. It was an awfully hard job to get her to give them back. Sadly, that same year, this lady was knocked down and killed by a bus.

During that year, we lost eighteen people—family and friends. It was the worst year of our lives. Up to Mum's funeral, I had not cried once, but after that, I just could not hold back the tears. That night, I laid in bed and literally sobbed uncontrollably. My beloved husband could only say: "Shut up, you silly!" There was no way I could stop and not in the least sympathy from him. Hence, I prayed, "Dear God, please help me to stop this sobbing."

Then I heard within me this beautiful, soft and caring voice say, "Peace be with you child. Know that I love you and that your mother is safe with me," and I felt such a beautiful, calming peace. That was something that I could never forget. And in times of sadness, fear or anxiety, I've always recalled that.

I kept my mum's flat on as long as I could so that my sister's children could still call in as they were accustomed to with Mum. For my brother Ted, it was a very traumatic time. He would sit up at the cemetery nearly every day for months. I guess, it may have been some kind of guilt, for most days, he would pass Mum's door to visit the pub and never call in to see her, which hurt Mum a lot.

My sister Jean also went through a very tough time of it. David's best friend, Jim, would knock on my door and say, "Pat, could you come and help Jean? She's in the pub again, singing her little heart out, absolutely blotto." So, off I'd trot, take her home and put her to bed. Eventually, Jean married David's best friend Jim and at the date of writing this (2008), they have been married for 40 years. She is a lovely person and I love her dearly. She now has five children; all grown up with good jobs, and Jean and Jim are proud of them.

Later in 1966, my husband, Tina and Tony, and I moved to St Francis Flats in a ground-floor flat. At one time, Mum lived there and one room was a little shop, which Mum ran, selling little children's clothes that Mum had made herself.

Now, it was returned to a three-bedroom flat. In March/April 1967, I was expecting our third child. I actually knew the very moment he was conceived. I often wonder if anyone else has had that experience and it was a wonderful moment, never to be forgotten.

On October 3rd, which was also my brother Terry's birthday, at 2:45 pm, my second son was born at the Elizabeth Garrett Anderson Hospital, Hampstead, London NW3. He weighed 6lbs 11oz. and was named Terence John Sidney. Terence was after my brother, John was my dad's second name and Sidney was my husband's father.

The next day, October 4th, my sister Jean married Jim. My husband was supposed to be there, but when police tried to find him, he wasn't there. Where was he this time? The reason he was wanted was that I had taken a turn for the worse and was extremely ill, so much so that I almost died.

A part of the after birth had been left behind which was the cause of illness. During the time that I almost died, I had a most wonderful experience. I found myself in a wonderful place, where there was perfect peace, and the most wonderful love surrounded me. I met my mother, who was dressed in the most beautiful green gown of very delicate material. There are no words to describe the colours that I saw. It was so wonderful to be re-united with my mum. We chatted not by word of mouth but somehow by mind, until I said, "Mum, how I would love to stay with you, but who would look after my baby? You know that my husband has no patience."

With that, I suddenly found myself back in the hospital bed with doctors and nurses trying to revive me. Shortly thereafter, I passed the remaining after-birth, and started to get well again. For many years, I never told a soul as I was sure that they would just laugh at me. But it was another experience that I would never forget. I knew, for certain, that we cannot die, we just change our form into what is known as the 'Spiritual Realm'.

The most profound thing was the power of love that I felt. I knew for certain that it was the power of God. I could never forget both: how beautiful my mother looked and how wonderful it was to see her. Many a time since I have wished that I stayed there, I guess, I'm having two lives in one.

Another thing that happened during the time I was in the hospital having Tony was that whilst expecting him, back in the 1960s, I had thrombosis in the left leg and phlebitis in the right leg. The doctor injected something into both legs but only one got better. After the birth, both legs developed a nasty rash, no way was I allowed to go home until they had healed. They were covered in this black tar stuff and other things, but they would not heal.

One night, this gentle voice I had heard at the time of my mum's funeral, said: "Child, ask if you can treat legs with Savlon cream." So, I asked and was made to sign a form to say that I had treated myself. I used the cream and my legs got better in no time. So, it is obvious that I have been truly cared for by God/Spirit in so many ways.

After Terry's birth, my husband asked me to keep my promise and move to the country. So, the wheels were set in motion to get an exchange council house to Ipswich, which was 17 miles from Colchester where my dad lived. I did morning and night cleaning of offices, to get the removal money together. I needed to save £200, which I did. My dad married his live-in partner in January/February 1968, Pat. My husband, our children and I moved to Montgomery Rd, Ipswich and Suffolk in September 1968. My husband suggested that I give him the removal money so that he didn't look a fool when it came to pay for the removal van.

He went with the removal van and I caught a train from Liverpool St Station to Ipswich. It was a very hot day and Baby Terry was very fractious. It was not an easy journey with three children, but we managed.

As we came out of the station, I can always remember that across the road, the hotel was painted blue and white, the sun was shining, and I felt happy to be starting our new life. I sensed it was a new beginning. I got a taxi to our new home, where Ron was waiting, and I expected that most of the furniture would be in and that we could have a nice cup of tea. No such luck was greeted by Ron, saying, "They won't move anything in until we pay them."

"Well, why haven't you paid them?"

"I've got no money," was the reply. I'd worked all those hours and nursed a new baby and not a penny was left. So, the removal men let me search through my coats in the wardrobes for enough money for Ron to catch a train to Colchester, to see if Dad could help out. I found just enough, which was eight shillings and Dad—bless him—helped with the cash. What Ron did with the money, God in heaven knows. I could surmise all sorts of things, and I don't think that I would be wrong, but we were here now and hopefully, we would stay as one happy family.

It was wonderful to actually have a house; no one above or below us, making noise etc. We had three bedrooms, bathroom upstairs and a hall, two rooms and kitchen downstairs, plus garden; front and back, an outside toilet, and, miracles of all, an outside shed. It was marvellous. The only thing was that it was bitter cold in the kitchen.

My husband seemed happy, and wonders of wonders, he seemed to have a special attachment to Son Terry. He loved playing with him, which he hadn't done with Tina and Tony. By this time, we had a car, which was a white Mini; very temperamental in cold weather. I had a few lessons in that. My husband got work as a taxi driver, using our car. But wages were not very good, and I did not want to work this time. I wanted to bring up my baby myself. Perhaps that was selfish of me, but I so wanted to be a proper mum to all the three children.

Having been evacuated during the 1939/45 war, I knew how important that was and, of course, remembered how I felt being parted from Mum and Dad.

Soon my husband started a new job; this time as a driving instructor (very silly of me to let that happen, in hindsight with his eye for the ladies). I just never dreamt that he would do it again. For a while, everything was okay. We had a Baxi Boiler behind fire, so had radiators fitted throughout the house, which was a God sent.

When we exchanged homes, we left our cat with the new owners, and they left their dog "Smartie" with us, as they were not allowed to keep dogs in the flats. So, it was marvellous for us all to have a dog. He was black, with lovely pointed ears, like a small Alsatian with a bushy tail. He was known to the police as Basil Brush, for he was always escaping the moment door was opened. We all loved him.

One of our first visits to a sea-side was to Aldeburgh, where my husband purchased fresh fish. The next day, I attempted to clean and cut it up to cook. I had never done so before. I went to cut into it and it moved. I rushed out of the kitchen and wouldn't go back until my husband came home. What a silly Billy eh, I must have hit a nerve.

Well, my wanting to be a real mum didn't last long for the next thing was that my husband was telling me that he had met someone else and was leaving the next day, meeting her at the station and was going, of all places, to London. We lay side by side that night, which is when he told me, and I cried so much. I couldn't believe it was happening again. I hadn't suspected a thing, for as a driving instructor, it took in day and sometimes evening work as well. It was absolutely devastating. I had no family or friends in Ipswich, and here I was; left high and dry and the children were inconsolable. (Could it be that here was an example of how "as you sow, so shall you reap", remembering the John episode).

Tony barricaded himself in his bedroom and wouldn't come out or even go to school, Terry cried a great deal, and poor Tina had to put up with a mum, who now had pneumonia which the doctor said was caused by shock.

No amount of trying to comfort the children seemed to work. I could not understand why it all came about. I had the husband of the woman who he had left us for, visiting and yelling and shouting about it all, and the children to try and comfort. Without a penny, other than family allowance at the time, a kind neighbour told me to go to social services, which I did, and this helped. We had no money for clothing the children so the social services sent me to W.R.V.S. to kit them out.

That was so embarrassing, especially when this lady, who perhaps thought that she was being kind, offered up a second-hand bra for me to try. Then came a time when my own father visited me to take away a carpet that belonged to my mother, which she had made me promise that I would never allow him to have, for he was also living with another woman, and she wanted my mum's carpet. I had no strength left in me to stop him from doing so, and off he went with it.

But the worst thing of all was that some kind soul reported to the social services that I was co-habituating with a man, which of course was my father. I was so upset that I told the social services what to do with the money. My neighbour was a foster mother, and she kindly offered to care for my baby whilst I went to work, doing office work. Each time I left my baby, I cried all the way to the bus stop. In the evenings and during the night, I would sew sheep-skin gloves and cover hangers. There were times when I didn't even go to bed in order to finish my homework, or even be able to eat to ensure that the children had their food.

Tina—bless her—helped me regarding the hangers by fitting the hook into the wooden handle. But alas, she got a rash. I telephoned the doctor and explained the rash, whereby he said, "I believe, she may be allergic to the wood. Give her one of your anti-histamine tablets and see what happens." Yes, he was right. That did the trick but no more help from Tina in that respect. Though I must say, she did help me as much as she could in many other ways.

Once during the pneumonia, the doctor gave me some foul medicine to help with depression, which worked wonders. I begged for more to keep me going, but he said, "No, you now have to learn to cope on your own."

I was used to going to church in London. Although I was baptised as a Roman Catholic like my dad, I didn't stay with that religion, for I could not believe in eating fish on a Friday and many other things, and was confirmed in London in the High Church of England. However, now I couldn't afford the bus fair to go into Ipswich, to my type of Church, and I really felt the need to be close to my God again.

I did not realise then that I did not need a Church, for God is with us, where ever we are and in all that we see, hear, feel, sense or touch. So, I went to the local Baptist Church. There I found healing words in all the hymns and much comfort in the addresses. It was as if it was all said just for me. The Rev. Harris had great compassion and was a great help. Once my husband had left, it was amazing what came out of the closet, so to speak. The woman he had left us for was not the only woman he had recently become involved with. He had also stolen deposits for driving tests; no wonder he had to leave.

He never once sent a single penny to help cope with the children's needs and left me to pay for any outstanding debts. I was quite friendly with one particular neighbour, but alas, I was now a threat; being a woman on my own, I may take someone else's husband, which was another painful lesson to learn. Occasionally, he would phone the children, which I resented very much. Why should he have that pleasure when he had walked out on them and never helped to keep them? Of course, I know now that it was unfair of me, but I did feel so bitter at that time. He wanted to see them on one occasion. I agreed but hated the thought, but as is the way of things, they all had colds and couldn't go to meet him. Naturally, I was secretly pleased; in hindsight, I know how wrong I was.

There came a time when I had found new friends through working. They insisted that I must get out and make a new life for myself. My daughter Tina also thought that I should do this. So, it was suggested that I should join the club for divorced and widowed people.

The day or rather evening arrived to do that, I got myself dressed up and set off for the bus stop, but once there, I bottled out and returned home to be told by my daughter that

I was a coward. Golly, how could I let any of my children think that about their mother and teacher? So, I set off again. This time, it was snowing.

I arrived outside the club but just could not go in. Eventually, a gentleman came out and started chatting, telling me that it was safe to go in, as everyone else was in the same boat as myself and would only be too pleased to tell me their stories. So, I would have no reason to think that others would not talk, or to feel ashamed. He turned out to be the chairman of the club so I ventured in.

He was right in no time; many people were telling me their stories and being friendly. The only fly in the ointment, so to speak, was that the husband of the woman that my husband had gone off with was there. He was so unkind and told me that I hadn't looked after all my husband's needs, otherwise he would not have left. I was so naïve that I didn't have the common sense to say, "Well, that is obviously what you did yourself too."

However, I quite enjoyed the company of other people, and it helped to know that I was not the only one in this situation. There was dancing, but the nice thing was that there was what was known as queue dancing. Ladies would queue, and the gentlemen took first in the queue, danced once around the floor and placed her back on the queue, which seemed very fair to me. That way, no one was left out. Of course, I sat out for a long while, just watching and then there came an interval where one could get a cup of tea or a cold non-alcoholic drink.

People sat around three sides of the hall, chatting and drinking, but only one man sat on his own in front of the stage area. I felt very sorry for him. Was it his first time here, just like me? He felt somewhat alone.

So I got him a cup of tea and joined him, only to learn many months later that he always sat there to make people feel sorry for him (cheeky, eh). However, dancing started again, and this man made a point of dancing with me much more than once around the floor and asked if he could take me back to my home on the back of his motorbike.

I agreed once I had discovered that he was a widower; his wife had died of cancer. Off we set on the motorbike, where I said home James home, which surprised him, as that was his second name. We became quite good friends. I remember on one occasion, he arranged to meet me outside a cinema in town together with his son. I waited where he said for an hour to discover that he was outside the other cinema. That was his thing; always doing the opposite to what he said.

The time came for me to go to court for the divorce, for now, I knew that my husband would never change. There would always be other ladies, though now, perhaps in hind sight, I realise that he was in so much trouble for the money he had taken that, of course, he felt he had to leave. (Wishful thinking; no, I do not think so, for he married the woman and is still married to this day).

Rev Harris came to take me to the court, bless him, but I told him that I couldn't go through with it, as in my marriage vows, I had married for better or worse. He really surprised me, for he said, "Does your father love you?"

"Yes," I said.

"Then, do you believe God to be your father also?"

"Yes," said I.

"Do you not think that God loves you enough not to let you suffer again?" he said. Wow, that really shook me; a priest believing in that way. So, I went ahead with divorce.

I was heartbroken really, for I truly loved my husband and as I was taught in church that one married for better or worse, and my children would have no father. I knew what that felt like, for I had been through that situation myself, regarding my own father and had promised myself that it would never happen to my children. But alas, it did, and there was nothing I could do about it, or was there?

For in 1971, actually 13 November, 1971, I married the gentleman I had met at the club, named Bob. And of all the things, we were married in the Baptist Church. Before we were married, there was one Christmas where I had hidden away Christmas gifts for the children, but sadly, they found them. I felt so sad for them that I bought all new gifts for them, which left us very short of cash and not enough money to buy a chicken for our Christmas dinner.

On the Christmas Eve, there came a knock on the door. It was Rev Harris. He said that congregation donated money each year to help people in my situations. It was wonderful of them. We were able to have all the trimmings for our Christmas Dinner. (You see, God has always provided for me, and I really knew that.) For a few years, I always attended that church near to Christmas and gave what I could afford to help others, as I had been helped.

My new husband insisted that we move into his home, which was a detached house in East Suffolk that he owned. Sadly, he was somewhat of a prude re council estates. I find that hard to understand: a home is a home, whether it be a tent or a house, or whoever owns it. We all settled down to a great extent, except that his son was very angry at having to share with a new family, which is understandable, but he did make my life, and especially his dad's, very difficult.

He was so very different from my three children. He had been completely spoilt, had a private education and really thought that he was above all my children. Plus, his own mother had passed due to cancer.

It was a lovely service at the church, and I remember young Terry coming up to the front and handing me a hymn book. Bless him, he didn't think that his mum had one. The reception was held at my mother-in-law's home. Bless her, she was a real dear. When Bob and I became engaged, she wrote me a lovely letter, thanking me for making her son such a happy man again, which was amazing really. Most mums would be concerned at that, taking not only a wife but three more children.

We always got on very well together, i.e. Mum Suson and myself. The only unhappy period was due to Bob's son. He really made our lives a hell, having said that one could also understand that he had been the only one in the family but now, there were four. Of course, my tinkers played up too, but there were things, like playing Bob and I, off against one another, but we soon cottoned on to that, and when they asked us individually for something, we always said that we would talk to one another about it and let them know. Mind you, Bob was renowned for saying 'No', then thinking about it and doing what he could. The children always had a giggle when we went shopping, for Bob had a favourite saying: 'two for price of one', so it had to be bought.

We had a lovely garden at our new house, where I was also able to grow strawberries. If I watched out of the boy's bedroom window, I would see Tony creep in from school and gobble them up.

All three children did well at school. Tony was in the Boy's Brigade for a while, then in Sea Cadets, before he went into the Royal Navy, and Terry was first in the Cubs, then the Sea Cadets where he won many trophies. Followed by Royal Marines, he gained his Green Beret and then into Royal Navy.

Once Terry started infant school and Tony started high school, we found it difficult having different surnames. So, Bob suggested adopting all three children. Tina was at the age where it would not be too long before she probably would marry, so she said that it was a waste for her to be adopted. But the boys agreed and it was set in motion. I remember writing to Ron about adoption and getting a reply to the effect that my new husband was sitting in his rightful arm chair, i.e. Ron's armchair; what a cheek, eh.

However, it all went quite well, and the adoption took place. It made life a lot easier; school and club wise. Now Terry had started school. I was free to work again if I wanted to. Soon, Bob came home and said that they wanted typists where he worked, so I started there at Ransome Simm's and Jefferies.

I used to meet a lady at the bus stop, who used to chat to me and tell me all her worries. We—Bob and I—became friends with her. She was divorced and had a little son. She also had a grown-up daughter, who at that time was out in South Africa, and her mother was very worried about her. But quite soon after this, the daughter moved to America, where she hoped to become an American citizen and then send for her mother and baby brother.

Sadly, she was epileptic and needed tablets for that but to become an American citizen, she needed a clean bill of health. She did not obtain the drugs required for her condition, and at the young age of 21 years, sadly, she died. Her poor mother was absolutely uncontrollable. We looked after her son for a while. Eventually, when his mum was a little better, we all went on holiday together.

One evening, we visited mum and son, whereupon, she handed me a rolled-up paper, tied with ribbon and said, "Please look at this and tell me what you think of it." Which I did, and I was flabbergasted. It was a beautiful pencil drawing of my grandmother. I could not understand how she could have it, for she knew nothing of my grandma, who had died at least 18 years previously.

Well, she said, "I went to a Spiritualist Church, where a psychic artist was doing private sittings. His name was Ivor James. I hoped, of course, that I would get something from my daughter. But he apologised and said that a lady would visit me in three days' time, and the drawing is of the lady's grandma, who would like her to try and contact her. I had one tiny photo of Nan at home, which I found up and lo and behold, it was truly my beloved nan. Due to that, I actually discussed with my husband what had happened.

When I had polio and meningitis, and what had happened after the birth of my youngest son, and the comfort I was given regarding mother's passing away and, of course, the glasses episode during my W.R.A.F. time. He told me all that his wife had seen just before her passing. We realised that this was all too much of a coincidence just to let it pass. So, after much discussion, we ventured to the Horley Spiritualist Church, 345 London Road, Ipswich. Both being very nervous, we sat in the back row.

It was a beautiful church, well lit; no sitting in darkness. Prayers were said and hymns were sung, and an address was given by the president and medium, Miss R.E. Wardle, which was extremely interesting. Then, she started clairvoyance, which was giving messages to people in congregation from their loved ones. I noticed that when we entered the church, on the platform was a beautiful display of flowers, some of which were pink roses, which immediately made me think of my grandma, for she had a rose arch that held the same coloured roses as was displayed. I instinctively knew that I would hear from my grandma, and I did.

It was the last message of the evening. The Medium Miss R.E. Wardle described my grandma, and how it was that she passed away. She also described my mother and how she had passed away and many other members of my family. I was amazed. Medium also told me that I had a red-leather purse that had been thronged by my mother. It was locked inside a tin, which was inside a cupboard and that the purse contained various little trinkets, plus a half crown piece, plus the date that was inscribed on it. I could not confirm the date there and then, but on returning home, I found it to be true.

It was 1926. The medium also said, "I never ever give this sort of message to a person, for fear of causing someone to do something that perhaps is not intended for them to do. But my guide informs me that I really must tell you this, and that is that one day, where I stand, so will you stand."

I thought that she meant that I would do clairvoyance also, so I said: "Oh, no, ma'am, I do not think so, for I am a very shy person."

"Be that as it may," she said, "but I assure you that you will."

Well, as we went into the hallway after the service, Miss Wardle beckoned me over to her and said, "You have a North-American-Indian guide with you. I was stunned and must admit that it somewhat scared me. "Do come again," she said, "for you have many gifts to develop."

Naturally, Bob and I discussed the service and were astounded at the proof that I had received. Hence, we attended the church as often as possible and continued to receive messages from other mediums, giving more and more proof of my loved ones, now in spirit, and of how I would be working spiritually. (That first attendance was the latter part of 1972.)

At that time, I was working as a typist and was typing repetitive columns of numbers, which caused me to have tenosynovitis; in other words, tennis elbow. So, I thought that I will try this healing thing out and see if it works. The doctor had said that I could be off work for a few weeks. So, I attended a healing session at the Horley Spiritualist Church, and lo and behold, it did work. I returned to the office within ten days.

On my first morning back, I said to myself, "Oh God, I wish I did not have to return to work yet, as I would like to continue reading a book that I had found in the church library, written by 'Ena Twigg', a famous medium." She mentioned so many things that had happened to her, which I could relate to as happening to me. I could not believe it that someone else had experienced the same things that I had and had kept to myself for so very long, for fear of others not understanding.

However, I had only been back to the office for approximately half hour, when I slipped on built up polish in the hallway and fractured my leg and tore the ligaments. This was early 1973 and the doctors said that I would not be returning to work until approximately December. So, I had all the time that I needed to read and study about mediums, as to how they worked. Thus, I was able to return to the healing group and was fit and ready to return to work in June.

The Healer Mr Basil Saunders used to give me messages from my mother that were absolutely correct. On one such was a warning from Mum, to say that we should check out our guttering because if it rained, we would find water entering through our kitchen window. Well, I told my husband, who pooh-poohed the message and said that it was nonsense.

Sadly, he would not check the guttering, and lo and behold, it rained and yes, the water did come through the kitchen window.

What we had forgotten was that there had been gales. Some roof tiles had to be replaced and in doing so, the work men had dropped some cement which had blocked the guttering.

So, that was concrete proof if ever there was proof needed. I sent that story to the Psychic Newspaper Office.

Whilst receiving healing, I felt very deeply for the other patients, and so I wanted to try and see if I could help in this way of healing. And I was very fortunate to be asked to join the healing team and discovered that I too had the healing gift. I loved healing; nothing else interested me. I did not seek any other form of mediumship, but the powers that be, decided otherwise. Whilst giving spiritual healing, I found that I too could give people clairvoyance and proof of their loved ones, now still living in a spiritual dimension. To see the pleasure that gave to others was so wonderful in my mind, and I was truly grateful to the spirit.

On the very first occasion that I entered through the schoolroom door—where the healing always in those days took place—at the church, I heard this very gentle voice in my head, saying to me, "This is your home." I thought that perhaps it meant that this is where I was to discover the truths that I had longed for, but no, in hindsight, I now realise that it was a fact, for in the year 1990, I did live in the purpose-built bungalow and became president of the church, so Miss Wardle's message to me, all those years ago in 1972, was also absolutely correct.

My husband, Bob, also later joined the healing team. But sadly, there came a time when he wanted us to give up the healing and attend the church. I explained to him that I had found my truth at last and I really could not do that. I would not give up the wonders and truths that I had found, and life, for the time being, settled down again.

Within a year, I was invited to do a service at the Felixstowe Church, which in that day was held in a garage. After which, I was invited to complete services throughout East Anglia, as far North as Huntingdon.

We—Bob and I—continued with the healing, and Bob joined me. When taking services, he would do the address, which he wrote and read. Every address had a beginning and an end. He was really good at that but for the life of him, he could not do it without reading it. But nevertheless, everyone enjoyed his address. I would do the prayers and the clairvoyance.

I was invited to join Miss Wardle's circle at the church, plus we started our own home circle. The North-American-Indian (that Miss Wardle had mentioned at our very first meeting) made himself known and said that his name was Running Bear and explained how he received that name. He also said that he would prove to me, at the church, his name.

So that particular Sunday that he had said he would give the proof, I attended the church, expecting to receive a message from the medium, but alas, the service ended, and I had not received the proof as promised. But a gentleman that was sitting in front of me turned around and said: "May I have a word with you?"

"Of course," I said, "yes."

Whereby, he said, "I have a North-American-Indian here, who asks me to tell you that his name is Running Bear."

Well, I was over the moon and so delighted; I'm a stickler for real proof you see. Now, the amazing thing is that for my 14th birthday, my mother bought me a record called "*Running Bear*". I also, via our circle work, discovered that the lady I had seen at my bedside, dressed in black, when I had polio and meningitis was my guardian angel, a mother superior in an order of nun's.

Also during our home circle, we used to have a Carmelite Nun come and talk called St Theresa of the Rose's. She explained that the white rose represented peace, the red rose was passion, the pink rose love, the yellow rose strength.

Now, on one occasion, we were about to go on a holiday when St Theresa said, "You will see me during your holiday." Well, bless me, on the way down to Cornwall, we visited Buck fast Abbey and visited a shop to buy ice-cream for our youngest son. Lo and behold, there stood on the floor was a statue of St Theresa, holding the roses in her hands. It was for sale for £25, so I spent all my pocket money and bought her. What a wonderful proof that was too (I have recently given her to my niece of the same name).

There were times when my husband, Bob, would be giving me healing and he would mentally ask a question, and one such as Abraham Lincoln would answer his question for him through myself. Bob had some wonderful proof from him. From all the wonderful things that took place in our home circle, I can never doubt the truth of there being a life after what we call death, life is truly continuous.

Our family life continued during all these exciting times, as did our working lives.

We had help from Bob's mum and from personnel at work, which led to Bob's son living at the YMCA. He became a much nicer person and met his wife-to-be there.

Tina left home which was heart-breaking. The police informed me that there was nothing that could be done as she was 16 now. I did not hear from her for a very long time. Then one day, I was shopping in Marks and Spencer's, where the assistant who served me turned out to be my very own long-lost daughter. We arranged to meet, whereby she told me that she had met someone else and wanted to get married.

Bob and I discussed the situation and invited her to return home, whereby she could save for her forth-coming marriage, this she did. We met her future husband, John, who was a very nice person. He became like another son to us, and they married. They had their reception at home with us and in later years, gave birth to our first granddaughter, followed by a grandson.

I feel that it is the right place to explain that since the breakup of my first marriage to Ron—Tina's father—I have always felt a kind of resentment from Tina to myself. I have no idea why it is, or what it is, and when I have attempted to ask her, she denies it, or says: "You chased me with a broom once." If only she could be honest, even if the truth hurts, it surely would help us both to come to an understanding. I personally do not need to feel continuously rebuffed, so hold back so as not to feel the pain. I so yearned to have grandchildren to love, cherish and spoil in a good way, but that has been denied to me by Tina.

So much so that I did not know even that I had a great grandson until he was nine years old. Plus, two other grandchildren, out in Australia. That said, now I must put it to one side for my own sake until hopefully one day, the truth may come to light, and all can be resolved with love.

It was not easy bringing three children up on my own, feeding them, clothing them, loving them, and working, also taking in homework to be able to make both ends meet, and going without food myself. But I am pleased to say that I did it, and never ever even considered leaving them or having them placed in a home of some kind.

Our two sons continued with their education, where they both were doing well. The youngest, Terry, was still in Sea Cadets, where he won many trophies. He was extremely smart. We invited his real father together with his new wife to one of his special parades. Whilst Ron and I were watching a particular part of the parade on our own, he cheekily made advances to me. I was flabbergasted; how could he; now that he was married to someone else. Some men have the cheek of the devil.

Tony left school and joined the Royal Navy, which had always been his heart's desire.

Ron and his wife were invited to his passing out parade. The cheek of the manmade advances to me yet again. I will not write what I had to say this time, nor will I say what Tony's reaction was to him.

Tony was eventually posted to H.M.S. Ark Royal. In the late-1970s, the ship made a return to the television. A major BBC documentary series called "Sailor" was made, showing life on board the ship. The theme tune for the programme was "Sailing" by Rod Stewart. The ship visited Fort Lauderdale, Florida between 30 May and 14 of June, 1978, and was decommissioned on 14 February, 1979. I watched all the programmes but never once saw my son.

We did not see much of Tony after that. For some while, he was busy living his own life and of course, courting. We kept in contact by telephone and by writing letters.

On one occasion, my husband, Bob, youngest son, Terry, and I were to go on a holiday to a place called Fairy Glen in Wales, after which we were to travel to Birmingham for Tony's wedding. A night before the holiday, I dreamt about the grounds of Fairy Glen. On the day of arrival there, the owner of the property was out. Due to the dream, I was able to tell the family exactly where everything was in relation to the garden.

Whilst staying at Fairy Glen, our son Terry became ill, continually being sick, naturally I was very worried and inwardly said, "God, what can I do, for we cannot take him to a doctor, in the way that he is?" My, goodness me, we were sitting in the lounge, reading my book which was written by Vivekananda, mostly relating to Sai Baba—an Indian saint, much like Jesus was. There was a knock at the door and the landlady came in and introduced Dr P. K. Guptre and his wife. They were looking for accommodation for the night and just called in on the off chance that they would be lucky.

However, he noticed my reading material and said: "I see you are reading about Sai Baba. Come out to dinner with us tonight and I will tell you our story about him."

"Thank you," I said, "but we cannot as our son is upstairs in bed and is poorly ill. We cannot take him to a doctor as he is continually being sick."

He said, "That's okay, my friend. I am a doctor, I will see him now and let you know my opinion," which he kindly did and reported back that we should give him a glass of water, after which he will sleep until morning, and the landlady will keep an eye out for him. Therefore, we could go out for dinner with him and his wife Una, and they would relate their story regarding Sai Baba.

Apparently, whilst living in India, Dr Guptre was a doctor in charge of a large tea plantation. He was due to go on a holiday. Since Una, his wife, had cancer, the holiday incorporated a visit to see Sai Baba, in hopes of Una receiving healing from him. So, they arrived at Putaparttito to see Sai Baba to find thousands literally there also waiting, a tannoy message was calling Dr Guptre's name to go and see Sai Baba privately.

Once there, Sai Baba said, "Dr, I have healed you before."

"No," says he, "I am here for you to hopefully heal my wife."

"Yes," said Sai Baba, "all in good time. I am telling you that I have healed you before."

Dr said, "No, never."

Sai Baba said, "Yes, I have. Last Christmas, you had too much to drink. Whilst trying to walk home, you fell in a ditch in the progress of having a heart attack."

"My God," said Dr. "Yes, that is true. I must thank you."

Una received her healing and was made whole. Sadly, since then, they have both passed over to new life.

Dr and Una became our friends and came to stay with us in our home. Seeing our plum tree, he asked if he may pluck a plum as he had never seen them before. I gave him clairvoyance which he clarified. We also took him to Horley

Spiritualist Church and Miss Wardle also gave him clairvoyance which was accepted as being so very accurate.

He then invited us to visit their Sai Baba Centre in Wolverhampton, where I was asked to give an address to a room full of visitors and to do the blessing, which is a small container that holds fire; this is encircled around the congregation. A teletext from Sai Baba in India came to the Dr after the service, relating every word that I had said in the address. It was all so amazing.

Regarding Sai Baba, thousands of people would gather daily to hear him speak and give his blessings. He too has now passed away, and sadly, I have forgotten when it is that he is to return.

We travelled on to our son's wedding in Birmingham, where Bob and I felt at a loss as the bride's mother was somewhat like my mother and planned it all herself. Whatever we suggested to do to help was rejected. But nevertheless, the wedding took place and was enjoyed by all. We returned home and Tony and his wife returned to Helston, where he was stationed and set up the marital home.

I recalled a little time later that Tony and his wife had a lovely, honey-coloured golden retriever, which became pregnant; they were thrilled. Tony was so excited, and each time a puppy was born, he telephoned us to tell us all about it. Sadly, the last puppy was born dead. Tony was devastated but eventually, buried it and called it "Sleepy".

Soon after this, there came the Falklands war, and Tony had to go there on the H.M.S Hermes. He related to us how he had to sign his last will and testament. How difficult that must have been for him. H.M.S Hermes was the flagship for this war. She left UK on 5th April, 1982 and returned on 21 July, 1983.

Naturally, this was a great worry. One of our circle members attended a Saturday evening of clairvoyance at Horley Spiritualist Church, whereby a medium said that someone in the congregation knew of a mother whose son was on his way to the Falklands, and that her grandfather wanted her to know that he would return home safely. That person, Wally, phoned me that night and asked if it was true that my grandfather was in spirit. When I said yes, he then relayed the message, which was a great comfort to me, especially as at one time, it was reported that the Hermes had been sunk. On contacting the Royal Navy helpline, I was told, "No, mother, it is not true. It's just a propaganda."

Knowing how I so loved my grandfather, it was such a comfort to receive his message. Grandfather also proved that it was him, by telling the medium that he himself was in the 1914-18 war, which was so true. Actually, he suffered from asthma, caused by being gassed during that war. I always hear from grandfather whenever anything special is about to take place.

The day came when H.M.S. Hermes carrying ours and others' beloved sons back to Portsmouth Harbour. What a wonderful day that was.

We travelled by car to Portsmouth, together with our large white flag, which was a huge white sheet with 'Welcome Home, Tony' written in large letters on it.

Nearing to Portsmouth, there were many signs posted for us to see as to exactly where we needed to be and where to park to meet H.M.S. Hermes. Nephew John and his family met us there, as did Tony's wife and also, Tony's own father and wife. We were amazed at the amount of people: 3000 in fact.

There were many fly pasts of so many different aircrafts, and also a 17-gun salute.

Norman Wisdom was there with a Bulldog, wearing a Union Jack flag. The Royal Marine Bands were playing music and much singing took place. The excitement was over whelming. It seemed to take ages for the ship to dock. All the sailors lined the decks and were able to wave to us and us to them. I was thinking to myself that I will never see him in this crowd, when someone touched my shoulder and said, "Have you seen him yet?" On turning around, I was amazed to greet my son. What a lovely long hug we had. He had not seen his wife yet, as she had moved forward, nearer to the front. It was a day I will never forget. Writing about it has brought back so many memories and the tears are flooding as I write.

The then prime minister, Margaret Thatcher, went aboard and spoke to Hermes' Captain and others and thanked them for all they had done. One lasting memory of that day was that Tony's wife had brought him new socks to wear, there and then, as his had all worn out during the war. I guess they all left so quickly that they had no time to re-stock the goodies that they would need.

Tony came to Horley Spiritualist Association Church, whereby he was given a message via Miss Wardle, the church's minister and president, in relation to a pilot of an aircraft that Tony knew, who had been killed during the Falklands war; proving yet again that how life continues after death.

Sadly, not long after Tony's return, it was discovered that his wife had met someone else during his tour of duty, hence a divorce.

He eventually met someone else and married again where eventually, a grandson was born; Stephen. Approximately around this time, Tony was posted to Ireland at the time of many horrible events. It is very sad to say that he was a much changed man. I spent through the night many times sitting up with him and listening to his anxieties. How I wish that those who send our boys out to fight would try it themselves sometimes. Surely, then all wars would cease. It plays havoc with their minds.

He came out of navy and found it hard to get a job in the Newcastle area where he and his wife lived but eventually found work as a security guard in London. We—Bob and I—had an S.O.S. from him. He needed £200 cash urgently. Off we set to London and gave him the money he needed. Somehow, within my being, I knew that I would not see him for a long while (6th sense, I guess). Lo and behold, we didn't.

A couple of weeks later, his now new wife phoned us, trying to find him (before he left Newcastle, he had stripped every room of house, ready to decorate same). Poor lass, she had tiny, young baby, no gas, no electricity, no money to pay rent or to buy food and the items needed for baby. She could not contact him no matter how hard she tried. We could not help her in that respect because we had no idea where he was either. All I could do was pray which I did, "Dear God, please help. I do not know what to do."

I explained the situation and the fact that we had no money left to be able to help Tony's wife and the baby. To my absolute amazement, the next morning's post brought a letter, containing a cheque for the sum of £5,000 from a business man I had helped over a period of a few years, healing wise (for I never ever charged for what I believed was a gift). Of course, grateful prayers were sent off immediately and off we set to Newcastle. Next day, gas and electricity was installed again, and Bob and I set about redecorating the home and cleaning the garden up. It took us a fortnight to complete, after which we had a few day's holiday and then back to Ipswich where we lived.

We still had no contact from Tony. It was an extremely worrying time, I eventually became so worried that I telephoned the local police. The officer advised me to wait a month and then if not heard, contact them again. Golly, was he telepathic or what, for a few days later, the telephone rang, and lo and behold, it was Tony, our son, reversing charges and phoning from America of all places. His visa had run out and he could go to prison. Would we send him money for him to be able to return home? However, I phoned an airport authority and was advised not to send money, and what to do so that we did not lose our money. A flight was arranged, all was successful, and he arrived home safe and sound.

He lived with us in our bungalow as by then we had sold our house to move to the bungalow. He was obviously extremely unsettled. His wife came down from Newcastle with the baby, whereby we hoped that they would reconcile but sadly, no. There was no nastiness, thank God, but yet another divorce took place, and he continued to live with us.

Tony soon found work in Ipswich, engineering. In between all this, our youngest son had finished his schooling, and he too wanted to join the Royal Navy. We arranged a party for him on T.S. Orwell, where he trained as a sea cadet. However, Terry did his naval basic training and just as we did with Tony, we attended his passing out parade. His real father did also—cheeky as ever, thinking that I still belonged to him (no way) and tried his usual way of chatting me up.

Eventually, Terry was transferred to Royal Marines for a while, where he passed with flying colours, so to speak, and gained his Green Beret.

Then, it was back to Royal Navy, where he became a petty officer "writer". He too did a stint in Northern Ireland. Here we go again, more worry. He too went to Falklands but on a hospital ship and it was peace time, thank God. (My memory recalls that Miss Wardell had told me many years ago that Terry would not marry until after he had become a naval officer, which is what happened much later.)

It is rather strange really now I think back that my two brothers were in Royal Navy and my two sons, but we were never invited to go aboard a ship.

Bob and I continued to go to Horley Spiritualist Association Church and give healing every Wednesday evening. I also joined National Federation of Spiritual Healers (N.A.F.S.H.). In those days, to do that, one had to supply the names of 15 people who had been healed, from which they would contact a few names to verify that all was correct before one was made a member. After that, I would be contacted to give healing to whoever contacted them that lived in my locality.

We also joined a healing group run by Dr Ian Pearce in a place called Diss, East Dereham, Norfolk. That was held once a week.

The patients mostly seemed to have cancer. At the end of a healing session, when patients had all left, the good doctor asked all healers to sit in a circle, and he would place his hands on each person's head and give them healing. One could actually feel the healing power come through his hands. Dr Pearce (now passed) also came to Horley Church, as invited by Miss Wardell and gave a lecture regarding cancer and the various approaches to it, inclusive of healing. The church was packed to capacity for this. Dr Pearce also wrote part of a book called *The Longest Shadow in the World* by Findlay Macdonald, Macmanaway and Pearce Findlay (1978), plus another written by himself; *One Man's Odyssey.*

Bob and I continued our healing at the church and conducting church services throughout East Anglia, plus helping with the two main events held each year at the church for fund raising. There was a garden party held in July, now called 'Garden Fete' and 'Christmas Bazaar', for the fund-raising events. I discovered other gifts that I did not know I had; like making flower arrangements, miniature Christmas trees, night dress cases in the form of crinoline ladies, even repairing old, worn out Christmas tree used for the Christmas Tree Service. I enjoyed it all. The Christmas Tree Service was now held in aid of the Ipswich and District Animal Welfare Service.

In those days, there was also a midnight service held on New Year's Eve, followed by a party. Miss Wardell always did that service, and the church would be packed by about 100 people.

Flowers on the platform were always displayed by Mr Jack Robinson and were truly beautiful.

On Good Fridays, we always had an afternoon tea, followed by a service, conducted by Miss Wardell. Food was supplied by the latter and members of the congregation.

In later years, a Good Friday service was held and conducted by those learning to become mediums. This is a most important thing to do.

Miss Wardell sold her home at 331 London Road, adjacent to Horley Spiritualist Association during 1981-1982, to have a bungalow built to the rear of Horley

Spiritualist Association building. This accommodated herself, being the resident medium, and her trusted friend and original co-founder and trustee of Horley Spiritualist Association, Mr Jack Robinson, together with private facilities for visiting mediums.

Bob and I helped her move to her new home; one other person called Nan McDonald also helped (she is now deceased). It amazed me to realise that out of all the hundreds of people that she had helped, no one else offered to help her move. From now on, I am going to call her Edna, as we became great friends.

Soon, Edna and Jack settled in their new home, together with the 13 cats. We used to go several times a week to clean her home and church, plus do the gardening.

In April 1985, I had a phone call from my stepmother to say that my dad was in hospital. "He had a heart attack but no rush", she said, "as doctors said that it was only a mild one and would soon be home again."

My son Terry was coming home on leave that day from Royal Navy, so we decided that we would go for shopping first and then set off to see Dad. Whilst shopping, I suddenly became aware that my dad had passed away. I told my husband, who said, "It's probably your imagination." However, we unpacked shopping and left a note for our son and drove to the hospital in Colchester, where a doctor took us to sister's office, who then told us the sad news that Dad had passed to his new home in spirit world. The sister said, "They are now washing your dad, then you can go and see him." I asked her if he had seen a roman-catholic priest, as he was a roman catholic, to which she replied, "No."

When we went in to see him; he looked wonderful with a smile on his face. I guess it was my mum who came to meet him, for I knew that he loved her dearly. I placed the sign of the cross on his forehead and said a little prayer for him. Several years later, a medium said to me, "I have your father here. He is telling me to thank you for placing the sign of the cross on his forehead and the prayer. I had never seen that medium before. Yet more proof.

On bank holiday, Monday August 1988, Edna phoned me and said, "I thought you were coming today."

"Yes," said I, "just running a little late."

"Right." she said, "can you make it soon, as Jack has had a heart attack and has decided that he wishes to return to the spirit today."

My goodness, what a shock! Can such things really happen? So, off we went to Horley Manse, where upon Jack asked Bob to escort him to the toilet as he felt somewhat unsteady, which Bob did. When Jack returned, he sat on the settee and asked the three of us to sit close by and send him loving thoughts, which we did. He then took a long inhaled breath and was gone to his new home in the spirit world.

What a miracle that was, something completely new learnt.

Although Edna knew that he was safe, she missed him terribly, for he used to do all the shopping and buying of fresh fish for the cats twice a week and supplying and preparing the flowers for the church, and, of course, was a great friend and partner and companion. They were not husband and wife type partners, just simply good friends. Though I know that he really loved her, as many others also did. Who would not, for Edna was truly a lovely person, and very respected by all who knew her.

Edna continued to be poorly, but would not have a doctor, no matter how we pleaded with her. A couple who attended the church called on us and told us that if Edna passed away, we would be in trouble for not calling the doctor. So, with Edna's permission, I phoned her doctor and explained all to him, whereby he said, "I know her well, and when she is ready, she will ask you to call me," and so it was, just as he said.

Over the months that followed, poor Edna had a few weeks poorly and a few feeling a lot better. We gave her healing and many of congregation sent healing thoughts to her also. We continued to run the church in Edna's absence. During one of her good bouts, I suggested that she should tell us the story of how "Horley Spiritualist Association" came about. This she kindly did, and I wrote it all down. It has now been posted on the computer site: www.HorleySpiritualistAssociation.

So, Jack Robinson passed onto a higher life on the 29th August, 1988. There is a flower stand dedicated to his memory in the church. Jack was a truly a wonderful healer and also became a remarkable medium in the last two years of his life. He created many beautiful floral displays in the church; this he did every week. He was quite a good cook also and baked cakes for the various events held throughout the year. Jack also went with Edna when she took other services throughout East Anglia. Previous to joining with Edna as an original trustee of Horley Spiritualist Association, he was a well-known photographer in Ipswich Town Centre. He was part of a large family who also attended the church.

His sister played the piano during the services, held every Saturday and Sunday, also for Good Friday Service and New Year's Eve.

His brother also played piano for special occasions, such as naming services (christenings), weddings, plus funerals. All occasions were enjoyed by a very large congregation.

Bob and I became very busy after Jack's passing, taking on all the duties that he usually carried out for Edna, whilst still looking after our own home and family. Bless her, Edna really felt the loss of her dear friend and trustee. And I surmise that she started to concern herself as to the future of the continuance of the church, for she made haste to teach me how to chair a service, conduct funerals, weddings and naming services. Plus, garden fetes, Christmas bazaars, Good Friday services, followed by afternoon tea and New Year's Eve service followed by happy parties.

On Monday evenings, Edna held her circle and Wednesday evenings were dedicated to healing.

The healing team leader was Mr Basil Saunders, of which Bob and I also joined, for really and truly, healing was my first love. To see a person brought back to good health, was marvellous. I became a member of the NFS Healers; to be able to do this in those days, one had to supply the names and addresses of 15 people who had been healed, and NFSH wrote to a few to make enquiries before one was issued with the certificate. Bob and I attended many of their lectures in London and surrounding areas.

As a chairperson, I was instructed to ensure that the hymns for the evening were placed on the hymn board, make sure that the clock was wound and showing exact time and that the date on the platform was correct. Then I had to prepare water jugs and glasses for the medium and chairperson, and ensure that there were hymn books put out for both the medium and the chairperson.

After those duties were carried out, one had to greet the congregation as they came in and ensure that someone was giving them hymn books. It was also the chairperson's duty to make sure that someone welcomed the medium and show them where they could spend a few quiet moments, i.e. in the medium's room, exactly at 6:30 pm on a Sunday and 7:30 pm on a Saturday.

The chairperson would escort the medium into the church and onto the platform, pour their water out for them, then stand at lectern and welcome the congregation and introduce the medium to them, after which the service began with a hymn.

The chairperson then invited the medium to open the service with a prayer, followed by the Lord's Prayer; the latter being said by all. Then the chairperson would announce next hymn, after which invite the medium to share his address with the congregation. After which, the chairperson would thank the medium for his/her address and explain that congregation's free-will donations would be accepted during the singing of the next hymn that completed.

It was then time for the Chairperson to explain to congregation that the medium would now endeavour to bring proof of life after death, by bringing to them details of a loved one that they would understand. All the congregation needed to do was to send love up towards the medium and answer them with a nice clear 'Yes' (indicating that they understood) or 'No' (indicating that they did not understand) when he/she came. This was known as clairvoyance. That done more often than not successfully, the chairperson, thanked the medium for their excellent service, then read out loud the healing prayer and explained that people could place names in the healing book of people who needed healing, which would be found on a table in the hallway after the service. After which the chairperson would announce any future events to be held in the church and the names of any person that had donated flowers on the platform in the memory of a loved one.

Then it was time to announce final hymn number, and again invite the medium to say a closing prayer, after which all sang the vesper. The congregation was asked to kindly remain seated until the medium had left the church body, where he/she would be escorted to the medium's room and given tea/coffee and biscuits. It was also wise if the medium arrived early enough to offer a drink before service.

The chairperson would ensure that someone would look after the medium, then the chairperson would stand in the hall and talk to whoever may have questions etc.

Wedding service: I had to see future bride and groom and discuss the hymns that they wanted and, of course, help them to decide on the type of music they required when the bride entered the church, plus discuss what type of flowers they required on the platform or elsewhere. Arrange for a rehearsal date and explain that they would need to arrange all, also with the registrar at the registry office.

The bridegroom would be invited by the registrar as soon as he arrived in church to see her/him in the medium's room and check that all details were correct etc.

The registrar would sit on the platform during the ceremony, ensuring that all the words were said exactly as provided in the order of the service. She/he would also need a glass of water.

Plus, explain where it was that would be wisest to have their wedding photographs taken, and where confetti could be used. A table and a chair had to be supplied on the platform for the registrar, whereupon the bride and the groom would sign the register after the service. The president of the church would conduct the service, standing in front of the lectern and bride and groom in front of her in the front row of seats, together with the best man and whoever was giving the bride away, plus the bridesmaids.

One also had to arrange for an organist to play the hymns and any music needed whilst bride and groom signed the register.

For all weddings, I would make rib-boned bows to coincide with bridesmaid's colours and place at the end of each row of pews. And make sure that all the gardens were neat and tidy and block paving free from all weeds. Invariably, weddings were held on a Saturday, so once all photographs were taken and congregation gone onto reception, one then had to recheck that all was ready in the church for the evening service, restocking toilet rolls etc. and ensuring that the hymns changed for the evening, and making sure that all was clean and tidy again.

I completed my very first wedding service in 1990; it still makes me laugh to this very day, for I promptly started the service by reading the funeral service; dearie me, what a very silly Billie. Fortunately, the bride and groom were friends of mine, so that helped me to overcome my embarrassment.

I also had the honour of conducting my own son's wedding ceremony in later years.

All details regarding weddings, naming services and funerals had to be entered in a register that was held in the office at the bungalow known as Horley Manse.

Funerals: Funeral directors would telephone the president and give the details of whoever had passed to the spiritual world and confirm the same in writing, together with dates and times of the funeral service. After which, the president would arrange to meet the next of kin and discuss with them the order of service.

The president/minister would lead the coffin into the church or crematorium, and once the funeral directors had settled the coffin, the directors and the president/minister would bow to the coffin.

The service would begin with welcoming the congregation and an explanation as to how spiritualists believed and proved that "Life continues after a passing" followed by an opening prayer and the Lord's Prayer said by all. After which, a hymn was sung or a particular piece of music played as requested in the 'Will'. Then, the president would give the eulogy unless otherwise requested that someone well known to the deceased do so. Perhaps also say a few words regarding spiritualism.

Another hymn or music would be played followed by the committal and a closing prayer.

It was extremely important to time every part of the service to be held, as unless extra time had been paid for at the funeral directors, only 25 minutes were allowed in respect of a service held at Horley Spiritualist Association Church. After that part of the service, the cortège would continue onto the crematorium or the burial plot, which meant that all had to be very aware of the time. In relation to a cremation, one would ask the family if they required the curtains to be closed around the coffin, if yes, at what junction they required that to be done, for there is a button to press on the lectern.

There was a great deal to learn in a very short period of time. A funeral service does not have to be conducted by a priest or minister, any person is permitted to do so.

Naming Services (Christenings): Parents of a baby child would arrange with the president/minister a date and time for the service to be held. Words spoken of how all attending were severally responsible for the child. A hymn sung, an opening prayer said, plus the Lord's Prayer said by all. The child's earthly name was given and blessed by scattering flower petals over the child's head by myself after which I would go into trance, whereby a sister of mercy would control me, give the child its spiritual name and a résumé of any likely incident that may occur in its early life. I would be holding the child throughout this procedure, and I am pleased to say that a child never once cried whilst I held them. I was told that they looked into my face and seemed to be mesmerised at to what was taking place. I thoroughly enjoyed naming services. (A well-known medium conducted a 'naming service' for myself and guess what, my spirit name was 'Buttercup', meaning of which was 'well-trodden' but always bounced back.)

Sometime during the latter months of 1989, Edna became quite poorly health wise. Both Bob and I told her that if she felt the need to phone us, we would be there to help in whatever way we could, and so she did. We packed a few belongings, and Edna suggested that we use Jack's bedroom, which was next to Edna's bedroom, should she need to call us during the night.

Our son, who was now divorced, stayed in our bungalow.

In August 1990, we had the sad time of having to agree to our lovely dog 'Shep'—a black and white collie— being put to sleep. Bless him, he could not hold his water due to kidney problems. The vet said: "If he was always clean, then he would now feel very unhappy at being unclean, therefore, it would be kind to help him pass to a greater world in a gentle and kind way." We agreed, but dear me, it was so sad for us and him.

During the first week of November 1990, Edna saw in her mind's eye a square light switch, and on it, the date November 8th. She—bless her—was so excited, for she believed that it was the date when she would pass to a greater world. I begged her not to get too excited as it could be 18 or even the 28 November. However, this did cause her to request a doctor. He duly came and arranged for a nurse to come too, plus an oxygen bottle and a mask, which enabled Edna to breathe more easily. (The nurse was also a spiritualist and knew Edna, so that was wonderful.) Edna passed on the 18 November, 1990, just before midnight, very peacefully.

One of Edna's favourite flowers was the arum lily. Shortly before she passed, I moved it to a part of a garden near to her bedroom window, so that she would be able to see it bloom. It normally bloomed in April to May, but now, it bloomed during the first week of November, in the year of 1990. I had an arum lily panel made in glass and placed in one of the upper windows of the church, in her memory.

Edna's funeral was held at the Horley Spiritualists Association Church. The service was conducted wonderfully by Bob Clarke of Hitchin Spiritualist Church. There was not a space to be found in the church, its schoolroom or the hallway and some stood outside.

The little tinker Edna arranged for her coffin to go directly to crematorium with only the co-operative funeral directors with her; all others stayed at the church for refreshments, simply because I had told her that that is what I wanted when my time came. It was very wise as it would have been so difficult for all to get out onto the London road. Edna looked so beautiful in her coffin, for dear Tony of the funeral service had her dressed in an outfit like that of a nun in blue and white colours—bless him for that.

Whenever Edna had a funeral service to do at the church, Tony from the funeral directors always sat in to hear her very interesting speeches.

The congregation, over a period of many weeks, donated to have a memorial placed for Edna, which had been thought up by her some weeks before she passed, that was four wooden carved angels and named "Faith, Hope, Charity and Love". I have given the newspaper cuttings re these to the current president. The gentleman, who carved them, had only ever carved one other bust. The carver now lives in Australia; forgive me for at the time of this writing, I cannot recall his name.

In the summer of 1991, Bob and I went on a holiday to Wales, somewhere close to the Mumbles, near Swansea. We visited a spiritualist church there one evening, whereby the medium was conducting a service in trance. He said, "I wish to talk to a lady and a gentleman who are here on a holiday from Ipswich."

No one else replied, so I said to him, "Maybe that is us."

"Yes," he said, "if your names are Bob and Pat?" He apologised, saying that he had to keep the message very short as his time had been called. He then described Edna and said that she asks me to just say the word Bailey's. My goodness, we could not have had more proof of Edna than that, as since approximately 1980, each time Bob and I went on a holiday, Edna gave us a bottle of "Bailey's" to take with us.

There are many items in the church that have been donated in the memory of loved ones, like the handles on the doors that divide church from the schoolroom, the clock on one of the church walls, the hymn board, flower pedestals and silver vases, these latter are held in the bungalow. There is also a lovely framed photograph of Miss Wardle in the hallway, donated by a passed trustee, Mr Francis Smith. There is also a painted picture of her on the platform, painted by a member of the congregation.

Mr Francis Smith was a long and trusted trustee. He actually had all the seats recovered in blue velvet, which were ex-cinema seats, bought by Miss Wardle some years previously from the town of Framlingham and kept stored in her garage. He also provided all the curtains in the church, again in blue velvet.

There is a lovely, true story regarding Mr Francis A Smith and his wife, Jean. They had been trying for years to start a family but to no avail. However, Miss Wardle, together with her healing guide Dr Light, gave both healing and in time, Jean gave birth to a baby boy. They were a very happy couple regarding this, and their doctor, named Dr Weiner, came to see Miss Wardle and became a visitor to the church also. I believe that there was a write up in the local press regarding this.

Sadly, that baby boy became a man and according to his parents, made their lives very unhappy, whereby there was a parting of the ways.

Bob and I continued to run the church as taught by Edna and requested by her in a letter.

Not long after Edna passed away, Bob began to get restless again and did not feel inclined to continue with same. Hence, we parted and divorced quite amicably but remained friends.

I married again, this time to Terry, who was also a trustee of the church. We parted, divorced and remarried again in April 2001 but sadly, not for very long. He had a vicious temper. It was a very difficult time. Sometimes, he would start an argument and end up leaving to live elsewhere.

One of those times, he attended the church on the rare occasion that I was unable to attend due to a cold. On that occasion, it was discovered that water was seeping through the ceiling in the school room, hence, he went onto the roof and sorted the problem and came back to the manse, together with others, as his clothes were soaked through, due to the bad weather at that time. The others left.

Needless to say, of course, I had to offer to dry his clothes which resulted in us getting together once more.

Life, for a little while, was much happier, but not for long; back came all the old tempers, whereby he would take himself off to sleep on a garden seat outside, or on a cold stone floor in the kitchen. On one such occasion, I did not know where he was hiding and sleeping. I asked my spiritual friends to be told: "He is in the medium's bedroom." Off I went to look as it was unnerving, not knowing. I turned the light on there, but no, I could not see him. Coming back, I went to bed and said to my spirit friends, "Sorry, but he is not there."

They replied, "Yes, he is. Try looking on the floor, between the twin beds." After which, I was sure that I heard him cough, so off I set again, and lo and behold, that is exactly where he was. He threatened me and said that he would kill me and then takeover running the church. Hence, I got dressed and walked down to the police station. Two officers came back to the manse with me. By then, he was in bed, pretending to be asleep in Miss Wardle's old bedroom.

They gently woke him. I do not know what they said to him, but once they left, he said: "They just took the rise out of me, Pat." However, he left the next day but before doing so, he did something that he had never done before, and that was, he cleaned the whole of the church. Every now and again, he would attend a service and remark in a loud voice that how dirty things were since he had left.

This time, I had all the locks changed for my peace of mind.

It was very lonely, living there on my own. I went through a very difficult time, feeling very low in spirit. I remembered Edna saying to me, "As you were there to help me, when you are in need, someone will come to help you." And so, they did. I felt so poorly, I could not eat or wanted to do anything and along came a lady who bought me a cooked meal etc. and gave comfort, for which I was truly grateful.

It was truly a very difficult time in that kind of situation. Feeling poorly or not, one still has to continue to do the usual things in relation to the church: doors to be opened for whatever is taking place, such as the healing night, circle and services on Saturday and Sunday evenings. Bob still remained a friend and visited about twice a week. He now owned a mobile home in Martlesham.

Bob used to bring me old newspapers, as we collected them at the church and the money they provided was donated to the blind. However, I was scanning through one, one day and came across a mobile home for sale, which I could afford to buy. I thought about it for a while and told Terry, who once more had made me believe that he had changed and so returned, and we had settled down again. He became violent again and was very cross about it. Once more, we parted and he left.

So I had a word with my lady friend and her husband (for he was a medium), and she had many office qualifications which were needed in running the church. They said that if the mobile home was still up for sale and I could buy it, then it was meant to be. And they would take over running the church. And so, they took over in 2002, being Mr and Mrs Paul and Carol Windsor.

Paul was to be the resident medium, which was the main ingredient needed for the future of the church and Carol, the president, for she had all the ingredients for the accounts that would be needed for the continuation of the Horley Spiritualist Association. I bought the mobile home and moved in.

Terry came back again, but it was not long before his very bad temper took control again, feisty cuffs took place, and I tried to hit back, but he was much stronger than me. In the fight, he broke a small oak stool, shoved me into a chair and screwed the stool leg into what he knew to be my painful left foot, and rubbed cheese biscuits down the front of my blouse. He then took himself into our small bedroom that contained a small two-seater settee and slept there for several days.

He continued to work, but as soon as he came home, the verbal abuse would start all over again. He demanded a rent book (which of course was not allowed, i.e. to rent one's property). Daily, the abuse got worse, so that one day, when he was at work, I called a kindly policeman I knew. I explained all, and he advised me to call the police the next time it started, as in his opinion, Terry would end up harming me very badly.

It took me ages to do so, for I wondered that it would harm his chances at work, for he had long service in that respect.

I tried talking to him calmly and suggested that he tried anger management or a psychologist, but he twisted my words and said that I wanted him to see a psychiatrist. Off he went again; more abuse. Whilst he was still yelling and shouting so loudly, I took courage and phoned the police. They were here like lightening. They asked him to phone his daughter, to see if he could go and stay with her for a while. Which he did, but was still being abusive.

The two lady-police officers said that they would stay around the area, as they felt that he would attempt to return. Yes, he did, but again, they made sure that he left and advised me to put his property in the porch, and then phone him to let him know and ask when he could collect them but to make sure I was not around when he called. So, this I did.

I was out with my friend Therese one day, sitting in her car whilst she was shopping. I sent my thoughts out to my beloved creative power of the universe whom I knew to be my beloved Father and Mother God, asking if it was at all possible that Terry would see the error of his ways, so that we could still be re-united. The answer came: "Child, if he realises that he is truly at fault, then maybe." But alas, every attempt I made to talk to him was rebuffed, so it was once more that we were parted and divorced, so very sad for I did love him dearly. Another divorce took place in May 2005.

Bob passed away in February 2005, the last of my brothers passed away in April 2005, and Terry, my now ex-husband, on the 30 December, 2005 in a road accident.

I continued to live in my mobile home and also continued to serve other churches throughout East Anglia, including Horley Spiritualist Association Church, until 2013, when I retired as a medium. The last service I gave was at Felixstowe Temple of Light.

I continued to take Carol out for a day or shopping and to any dental appointments she might have, as her husband, Paul, was working and she could not drive. Suddenly, Paul—the resident medium—became ill. I would drive them both to the doctors' appointments and stay with Paul whilst Carol carried out church duties. Then in the August, that really well-loved man passed to a greater world. He was such a lovely man; everyone loved him and was such a very good medium also.

I continued to take Carol for shopping every week and helped with such things as the garden fete, Christmas bazaar and keeping the church gardens tidy and block paving weeded, clearing leaves etc.

From 2002 until February 2015, I remained as an honouree life president of the Horley Spiritualist Church.

Now, it is that I can no longer drive a car due to Macular Degeneration of eyes. I have had the pleasure to help a dear friend to develop his gift of mediumship, and he is now carrying out his duties in that way throughout East Anglia. He is part of many others who are to be the light workers of this world—helping to bring real truth, love, peace, and light and hopefully, save the world from destroying itself.

I am also helping others to develop the treasured gifts they have, for every single one will be needed to bring the help required to save this earthly world from destruction.

Of course, it is not easy being unable to drive any longer, and I am very grateful to those neighbours who help me out by taking me shopping and, on occasions, to a car boot sale etc. Plus, the friendship of my very special friend Therese and her partner Brian. I only have to say that whatever my need maybe, they are here for me.

Now, except for nieces and nephews; two sons and a daughter who do not contact me and have not done so for years, though I did make contact with my daughter, who now had a stroke. Therese, Brian and I visited her, and she agreed that should anything happen to me, she would be unable to help, therefore, she gave Therese her blessing to deal with whatever my need would be.

My whole family have gone home to the spiritual world and I am looking forward to meeting them soon and enjoying a wonderful get together and party, even my brothers and sisters have gone before me; them being younger than myself.

And there you have it, my friends, "The Fete of my Soul", as requested by my spiritual guides many moons ago. For it is that my guides chose the title, I will know why when I return home to the land, I know is a place of the most perfect love.

My spirit guides, also way back in the 1970s, arranged a gift for me to remind me that I was to write my story. That gift was a red-quill pen in its holder. That I still have to this day.

Appendage

And so, it is that the tides have come in and gone out and cleared the beach of all the past rubbish.

So, what is it that I have learnt over the past 82 years of earthly life?

Well now, in my opinion, there really is a creative power of this universe, which is known to me as 'Father and Mother God'; a power of absolute perfect love.

And that whatever hurt others may try to cause me, there is nothing that I need to do to counteract it, as there is a natural law that exists, that states: *"as you sow, so shall you reap"*.

No God will judge us; we do that for ourselves, for the God that I know is an absolute POWER OF LOVE.

Therefore, from all the proof that I have received from many different mediums, regarding family and friends, plus my own experience of almost dying, I now know for a fact that life exists after death, which leaves me with no fear of death whatsoever. So that now, I am looking forward to my rebirth into a beautiful home of pure love, light and joy.

I could write a great deal more, but sadly, my eye sight is failing quite fast, hence I am rushing to complete my true life story.

Blessings to all the past and present family and friends!